A Star-Bright Lie

Also by Coleman Dowell

One of the Children Is Crying

Mrs. October Was Here

Island People

Too Much Flesh and Jabez

White on Black on White

The Houses of Children

COLEMAN DOWELL

A Star-Bright Lie

Foreword by Edmund White

Introduction by Linda K. and John R. Kuehl

Dalkey Archive Press

Two chapters of this book first appeared in *Bomb:* #10 (Fall 1984) and #13 (Fall 1985).

The photographs by Carl Van Vechten are reprinted by permission of the Estate of Carl Van Vechten. The other photographs are reprinted by permission of the Estate of Coleman Dowell.

Library of Congress Cataloging-in-Publication Date

Dowell, Coleman.
    A star-bright lie / Coleman Dowell ; with a foreword by Edmund White and an introduction by Linda K. and John R. Kuehl. —1st ed.
    Includes index.
    1. Dowell, Coleman—Biography. 2. Authors, American—20th century—Biography. 3. Van Vechten, Carl, 1880-1964—Friends and associates. I. Title.
PS3554.O932Z47   1993   813'.54—dc20   92-30873
ISBN 1-56478-022-8

First Edition

Partially funded by grants from The National Endowment for the Arts and The Illinois Arts Council.

Dalkey Archive Press
Fairchild Hall
Illinois State University
Normal, IL 61761

Printed on permanent/durable acid-free paper and bound in the United States of America.

Contents

Photographs follow page 74

Foreword

When Coleman Dowell committed suicide in 1985 he was working on this book about his by-then distant memories of a disastrous theatrical career in the 1950s, but what he didn't appear to realize is that it reveals so many of the reasons for which he would kill himself. As should be evident to even the most inattentive reader, this book could be subtitled "Social Notes of a Hermit," for Coleman Dowell, even when I knew him in the last decade of his life, was both compulsively gregarious (curious, kind, hospitable) and deeply distrustful (easily wounded, unpredictably hostile, almost always disappointed by human contact). He was also fearfully shy, a trait not immediately apparent in a man so tall, handsome, sophisticated, and radiant.

I met Dowell in the mid-1970s after I wrote a mostly favorable review of his gnarled postmodernist novel *Island People.* I call it "postmodernist" because it plays tricks with point of view, the level of reality and fantasy, and the wavering reliability of its various narrators, some of whom were the masks of yet others. Reviewing it cold on a two-week deadline was a bit like working out the literary references after a first reading of the newly published *Ulysses,* but I now see that all those shifting perspectives beautifully deployed Dowell's own inner contradictions. When in fiction he could impersonate many different people he could dramatize and slow down his alarmingly busy thoughts. In real life, however, when he was obliged to express everything he felt with just one voice and in conversational order, he would become tongue-tied, he would stutter and finish sentences with a helpless hand gesture or almost inaudible suspension points. . . .

Similarly, in *A Star-Bright Lie* when he's forced to speak in his own right (that most baffling of all acts of ventriloquism) he has a hard time keeping pace with and notating his fragmented thoughts and shifting moods. I've seldom known someone so victimized by his own complexities. Some of them come through on the page—his paranoia, his bedeviled fascination with glamour, his lyric response to nature, his nostalgia for a Kentucky he'd fled and then reinvented, his bawdiness, his Gothic sense of horror, his touchy pride, his passion for black men, his alienation from both heterosexual society and the two forms of gay life he'd known: first the martini-swilling campiness of the fifties and then the triumphant machismo of the seventies.

The theater is one of the most sociable of all the arts and writers usually get their first plays on because they're schmoozers good at hanging out and chatting up. Dowell was too highly strung to do anything of the sort unless he was thoroughly drunk, by which point he could easily become abusive or incoherent. He was also too alert to grace notes, overtones, and ironies to be able to flatter the crude, debased, theatrical taste of his period. What's especially heartbreaking in *A Star-Bright Lie* is to hear how this great stylist, whose novels will be known to connoisseurs a hundred years hence, keeps dropping names of Broadway nobodies who've already been forgotten and who will be relegated to footnotes in future scholarly editions of this curious, truncated, unhappy text. His stars are our asterisks. For serious readers he's already far more esteemed than the people he writes about, with the sole exception of Isak Dinesen, although in his pages she is less an observed subject than an occasion for youthful chagrin.

I call his book "unhappy" even though Coleman intended it to be a lighthearted, scandalous romp, a shocker that would win him the big sales his somber novels had been denied. There again the theater and television corrupted him because they'd given him a hit-or-flop mentality and taught him success means big bucks and sidewalk recognition. How could the esoteric world of serious fiction ever give him a triumph of the sort he'd been led to expect?

When I knew Coleman he seldom emerged from his big, sunlit apartment that looked down on Central Park. There he'd receive people for dinner and give them quite simply the best food I've ever eaten—better than the food at Jamin or Lucas Carton or L'Archestrate or L'Ami Louis or the Tour d'Argent and far more varied, for one night it would be a *rijsttafel,* another a *feijoada,* a third Kentucky fried chicken made according to the elaborate dehydration and deep-lard frying method of yesteryear. Once, guilty about the effort and expense he went to in his preparations, I told him I'd come to dinner only if he would serve hamburgers and potato chips. He obeyed the letter but not the spirit of my law: he *baked* the buns, *puréed* the catsup, *sliced* and *fried* the potato chips, probably *pickled* the cucumbers.

Evenings at Coleman's were long, even very long (one early departure earned me a denunciation delivered in this book). They started with cocktails and his handmade pâtés, moved on to the narrow refectory table and its anything but monastic fare, and ended up with Coleman playing his own tunes on the piano. He spoke in a deep baritone, which alternated vanishing sentences, embarrassed stuttering, and startling stentorian cries of disapproval, outrage, or just frustration, as though if he could only shout his tongue might come untied—but he sang fluently in a dapper, unsupported tenor voice. Like many composers he splashed notes around more than he played them, but his voice and piano were adequate to rendering ballads as sweet and conventional as his novels are frightening, disabused, and permanently new.

After the concert Coleman's lover would walk the dog one more time and go off to bed. It was then, after midnight, that Cole could turn into an ugly drunk, bellow his rage and denounce everyone or become coolly sure of his visitor's iniquity ("You don't like me or my books, do you?" was a typical question). In my case he'd remember the few mild qualifications with which I'd seasoned that *New York Times* review I'd written before I'd known him, and he'd bring up each criticism, memorized and believed, whereas the praise had been dismissed and forgotten. The next day, of course, he'd ring up to apologize for anything he might have said that was *beastly* (he punched the one word *forte* in his otherwise *piano* sentence).

Whereas in Gothic novels the dire events usually happen at night, in Cole's life they happened by day when his lover was away and his next dinner still only in the *macerating* stage. It was during the day he'd descend from his sparkling aerie and stage raids on the homeless or unemployed black male population wasting time in Central Park. Or he'd concoct love letters to prisoners who'd advertised for pen pals. Or he'd pamper and scold his dachshund Tammy or, after her death, his terrier Daisy.

Once I read that the greatest love of Emily Brontë's life was her dog, which she'd beat, then nurse back to health and on which she apparently based the character of Heathcliff. Cole's feelings for Tammy reached similar dimensions. He bought her a fur coat and diamond jewelry but thrashed her when he thought she was dying on him. He once told me most of his female characters, the human ones, were derived from his tormented feelings over her. It was by day that Coleman conducted his violent affairs, canine and human. When evening fell his lover would come home from work, the apartment would be impeccable, the guests would be arriving, and Cole would be unsealing the venison daube that had been bubbling for twenty-four hours.

At those dinners Coleman entertained literary critics or such brilliant avant-garde novelists as Walter Abish and Gilbert Sorrentino or younger gay writers I'd brought to him such as George Whitmore and Christopher Cox (now both dead of AIDS). He basked in their admiration, although he was too fidgety, too suspicious ever to "bask." *Baste,* rather. Cole had cooler, respectful, but more distant relationships with such old-timers as Jack Dunphy and Tennessee Williams. And of course he had women friends, usually dancers or actresses or aristocrats, and with them he'd launch into bawdy sex talk and intimate quizzing that would shock them, embarrass him even more, but also flatter them. At least they weren't being treated as pals or little sisters, as gay men tend to do.

Food was perhaps a substitute for travel. Every dinner re-created with inspired intuition the cuisine of another country. He'd been to Europe a few times, but the memories of those trips remained pale beside his highly colored fantasies about Italian gigolos, French nobles, randy English eccentrics. Cole, of course, was an American eccentric in the tradition of Edgar Allan Poe, Wallace Stevens, and Joseph Cornell, those stay-at-homes who lived in a continuous waking dream about Europe.

Coleman had no normal or offhand way of treating people. He had only one mode—passionate. He wrote his nervous, muscular prose with passion. He gave dinners with a haggard devotion more appropriate to serving a jealous god than fickle friends. He loved his dogs and prisoners with passion and hated his literary enemies (most of whom were unaware of his existence) with poisonous rapture. His marriage was also a consuming, year-round, long-run passion play. Since his lover was Jewish, Coleman chose to be anti-Semitic. Since his lover was calm and reasonable, Cole was extravagant and irrational. Since his lover lived for Cole alone, Cole took up with one demon lover after another, although the entire act was played out before the admiring eyes of an audience of one—or two, counting Tammy. In an era when middle-class people aspire to well-regulated relationships that are sexually, morally, and emotionally expressive to just the right degree, Cole and his lover ignored such utopian precepts and contented themselves with a love worthy of Wagner and King Ludwig or Bacchus and Pentheus, i.e., one as destructive as it was deep and transfiguring.

At one point Coleman wanted to call this memoir "A Dark Book." If it is both dark and star-bright it's because his talent was as brilliant as his spirit was tragic. This unfinished book isn't quite the right vehicle for his genius. His novels, with their black pools of consciousness, are the best form for reflecting the white filigreed architecture of his inventive mind. No matter. Even a flawed work by Coleman Dowell is an occasion for celebration.

EDMUND WHITE

Introduction

Our friend Coleman Dowell was born in Adairville, Kentucky, on May 29, 1925, the fifth of six children. His father, Morda, a blacksmith/farmer, experienced deep bouts of melancholy that, according to Coleman, affected the latter's life and work, yet he admired this often frightening man. His mother, Beulah, was a good-humored, submissive, and gentle woman. Happy to be part of a "very beautiful family," he described his life with his parents and siblings as warm and loving. However, his childhood was less than idyllic. At the age of five, Dowell was repeatedly raped by a neighboring relative's adolescent handyman, a nightmare later relived in his novel *Island People*. This event, the most traumatic in his life, turned him into a passionate defender of the helpless—children and animals.

As professional model and master chef, Coleman seemed to be the epitomization of New York sophistication, but he freely acknowledged his provincial roots, including "a farmer's walk" and a rural school education. Even so, his real education was non-institutional, for the autodidactic Dowell children shared music, poetry, Shakespeare, the Bible, and, above all, the Kentucky ballads their Scottish father collected, ballads which, Coleman insisted, influenced everything he wrote. Moreover, in a favorite aunt's library, her favorite nephew, a lonely, imaginative child, became a voracious reader, encountering Becky Sharp, Emma Bovary, the Lintons, the Earnshaws, the Ushers, Gil Blas, Baron Charlus, Grendel, Piers Plowman, among others. He continued to read nineteenth-century English novelists for pleasure throughout his life, since they shared with him "a rage for order."

After graduation from Simpson County High in Franklin and a short stay in Cleveland, Ohio, Dowell entered the army and was sent to Manila, where he helped prosecute Japanese war criminals. While there, he attended the University of the Philippines "the way Gatsby attended Oxford." Returning home during 1946, he settled in Louisville for a few years as a full-time member of the National Guard. At the Armory, Sergeant Major Dowell wrote *Haymarket*, the unpublished musical play that brought him to the big city, as if he were Lionel Trilling's archetypal Young Man from the Provinces.

Arriving in New York, he said, "Well, I'm home." Coleman was now ready to begin the decade-long theatrical career (May 1950–May 1961) recounted in *A Star-Bright Lie*. The successful audition of *Haymarket*, which featured a love affair between a white woman and a black man, and which one spectator, Tennessee Williams, considered a ravishing work of art, led to various dramatic enterprises. First, Dowell became songwriter/lyricist for the DuMont Television Network's weekly program *Once upon a Tune*, composing hundreds of songs for personalities like Beatrice Arthur, Alice Ghostly, Charlotte Rae, and his new friend, Elaine Stritch. Next, as producer David Merrick's "Golden Boy," he collaborated with John Latouche on an abortive musical version of the Eugene O'Neill comedy *Ah, Wilderness!* Two years later, during 1957, he met Carl Van Vechten and immediately joined the exclusive Van Vechten circle satirized in the section of *Island People* titled "UP AT CLAUDO'S / A *Remembrance.*" Unfortunately, Coleman's adaptation of Van Vechten's 1924 novel *The Tattooed Countess* flopped at the Barbizon-Plaza Theatre in May 1961. He tried playwriting again, but dissatisfied with the 1965 Chelsea Art Theatre production of his original script *Eve of the Green Grass,* starring another friend, Kim Hunter, he turned at age forty to fiction.

Five conceptually and formally intricate novels emerged over a fifteen year period: *One of the Children Is Crying* (Random House, 1968), called *The Grass Dies* in England (Cassell); *Mrs. October Was Here* (New Directions, 1974); *Island People* (New Directions, 1976); *Too Much Flesh and Jabez* (New Directions, 1977); *White on Black on White* (The Countryman Press, 1983). Composed when Coleman was middle-aged, they are not "developmental"; indeed, the first four were engendered concurrently: "[W]hile I was writing *One of the Children,* I started *Too Much Flesh and Jabez,* finished *One of the Children Is Crying,* gave up *Jabez* and started *Island People,* stopped that and wrote all of *Mrs. October Was Here* in six months, went back to *Island People,* finished it, then back to *Jabez.*"

These works reflect their mode of composition. The motif of fragmentation, which dominates *Island People*—"ALL THERE IS, IS FRAGMENTS, because a man, even the loneliest of the species, is divided among several persons, animals, worlds"—had already surfaced in *One of the Children Is Crying,* where earth/air/water/fire are symbolized by the siblings, and in *Mrs. October Was Here*, where the characters stand for various aspects of the creative personality. It appeared again in *Too Much Flesh and Jabez:* "Thinking to have found herself in one character [Miss Ethel] would, without warning, 'become' another." Yet each fiction remains unique, for the 1968 work is a socio-psychological study of family life; the 1974 work, a satirical fantasy about revolution; the 1976 work, a cross between confessional tale and architechtonic novel; and the 1977 work, a framework narrative of sexual repression. Written separately, *White on Black on White* might be regarded as a docu-novel that explores racial relations.

Coleman, who was a critic as well as a novelist, reviewed books for the *Louisville Courier-Journal* from 1978 to 1981, praising the achievements of Gilbert Sorrentino, Edmund White, and others. The accolades his own creations deserved were slow in coming. Only *One of the Children Is Crying* was widely reviewed, perhaps because it had a large commercial publisher, appeared earlier the same year in England, and employed a less experimental mode than his subsequent fiction. Two comments characterize the generally favorable reception: a review in the *Cleveland Plain Dealer* said, "No one who professes an interest in contemporary literature can afford to miss it," while a critique in the *Irish Times* called this first novel, "a tough, uncompromising book . . . a masterpiece." Six years later, though, the reactions to Dowell's splendid second novel, *Mrs. October Was Here*, were so meager that New Directions had to quote obscure endorsements on its advertising circular. *Island People* fared somewhat better, for now testimonials from eminent writers like Tennessee Williams, Walter Abish, Ihab Hassan, and Gilbert Sorrentino could be cited. Though *Island People* attracted fewer reviewers than supporters, *Commonweal*, which termed it "a brilliant . . . allegory," and the *New York Times,* which designated it "a work of art . . . original and difficult," brought the author and his chef d'oeuvre to national attention. Not for long, however, because there followed *Too Much Flesh and Jabez,* Dowell's least reviewed work. One notable exception was the Sorrentino piece in the *New York Times Book Review* commencing, "This novel is a meticulously and subtly composed tour de force on the imagination." Published after a six-year hiatus, *White on Black on White* received more notices than any Dowell text since *One of the Children Is Crying.* They ranged from the negative response registered by *Kirkus Reviews,* which began, "There is no doubt that this book is the worst that I have been given to review," through the mixed response registered by the *New York Times Book Review,* which ended, "[I]ts psychological acuity, political insight, ferocious energy and authenticity of place partly compensate for its narrative awkwardness," to the positive response registered by the *Times Literary Supplement,* which observed, "He writes with a superb power of constant implication. . . . The book touches greatness."

Despite the fact that the *Review of Contemporary Fiction's* Fall 1982 issue devoted half its contents to articles on Coleman, including pieces by White, Sorrentino, and Thom Gunn, his audience remained small. What Robert Prager asserted in the *San Diego Gayzette* succinctly summarizes Dowell's literary standing before his suicide on August 3, 1985: "[A]lthough he is not widely known or widely read, it is already possible to speak of a Coleman Dowell 'cult.' Two of its most enthusiastic members are Edmund White . . . and poet Thom Gunn. Highly marketable writers themselves, they look up to Dowell as one of the living masters of American prose. Some day perhaps the public will catch on. Until then, he really is, as Tennessee Williams said, 'too good to succeed.' "

On November 3, 1985, Coleman's admirers gathered in the Fifth Avenue apartment he had long shared with his companion and literary executor, invited there by the latter to celebrate the life and work of his beloved friend. The crowd who congregated on that raw Sunday afternoon represented a cross section of many of the creative arts, fittingly so since the deceased was himself a gifted composer, poet, playwright, novelist, critic, teacher, model, and chef. They included Tamara Geva (dance); Walter Abish, Jack Dunphy, Lois Gould, Ann Lauterbach, Bradford Morrow (literature); Jack Beeson, Elizabeth Rich (music); Roger Baker, Balcomb Greene, Maurice Sendak (visual arts); Cecile Abish (plastic arts); Bob Emmett, Betty Low (theater); Deborah Baker, Peter Glassgold, James Laughlin, Leslie Miller, Betsy Sussler (publishing); the Kuehls (teaching). Among many tributes was the message Gilbert Sorrentino sent from California: "He was a friend to me and to Victoria for some dozen years, and his books, which testify to his brief reality, are part of our reality." Another encomium, Ann Lauterbach's "Uneasy Requital for Coleman Dowell," appeared in the Winter 1985 issue of the *Paris Review*.

Conjunctions and the *Review of Contemporary Fiction* each dedicated an issue to his memory within a year of his death. Soon afterwards Weidenfeld and Nicolson published *The Houses of Children: Collected Stories* (1987). Virtually all of these tales had appeared earlier in three different journals—*New Directions: An International Anthology of Prose & Poetry*, the English quarterly *Ambit*, and *Conjunctions*. Bradford Morrow, editor of *Conjunctions*, appended an insightful postscript to the collection: "I can think of few contemporaries who combine in writing the formal angularities, the sheer effulgence of word and phrasing, the Gothicism, the tenacity—almost inhuman in its deliberate gaze upon what we may consider so violent, so radically disturbing that we would wish not to glimpse it at all—and the authority present in this work." Simultaneously, the same firm reissued *One of the Children Is Crying* as a paperback. Reissued by the Dalkey Archive Press also during the spring of 1987 was Coleman's fourth novel, *Too Much Flesh and Jabez*. In 1990 Serpent's Tail published a revised and corrected edition of *White on Black on White*.

Shortly after his friend's death, the literary executor found an unfinished autobiography tentatively titled "A Dark Book." This discovery did not surprise him because *Bomb* magazine had already published one section, "At Home with Drosselmeier," and was about to publish another, "A Handful of Anomalies." The earlier piece treated Carl Van Vechten and his group, while the later piece focused on the Broadway world of David Merrick and John Latouche. Internal evidence places the time of composition as 1984, just one year before Coleman died. Obviously, then, he lived only long enough to complete the theatrical portion of "A Dark Book." The concluding passage, where the author "address[es] the theater directly in [his] own terms of disillusionment and impotency," contains a song, "No You, No Rain, No Rose." The title of these memoirs comes from the second stanza of this song, for it was felt that the following lines describe more vividly what Coleman Dowell experienced as a New York playwright than does the vague "A Dark Book":

Linda and John Kuehl

Now I can read high above me
When moonlight brightens the sky
The ways you told me you love me
And each word you wrote is a
far, bright,
A star-bright
Lie.

LINDA K. and JOHN R. KUEHL

The manuscript of A Star-Bright Lie *is located in the "Coleman Dowell Archive" at the Bobst Library (Fales Collection), New York University, which also houses 200 pages of typescript materials for an unfinished novel, "Eve of the Green Grass," 1,000 pages of Dowell's private journal, dated 1964-1984, and other important papers.*

A Star-Bright Lie

Prologue

I have been a visitor to New York only twice in my life, both occasions of high joy. The first time I came was to play an audition of my musical *Haymarket,* an audition that had been arranged by a traveling salesman who passed through Louisville and heard my songs at a party. The day before his letter came with the surprising news, I had dropped into a trailer parked in St. Matthews, Kentucky, where I was a civilian employee of the army, frozen by the trouble in Korea in my job as sergeant major of the 149th Infantry Regiment of the Kentucky National Guard. (Until mobilized, guardsmen are civilians, though I always wore my uniform on the job.)

The sign on the trailer was a modest one: PALMS READ. Inside I found an unexotic woman, a housewife with a Midwestern accent, who told me that I would receive a letter almost at once which would effect a large and lasting change in my life, though the change itself would not occur for a few months. It seemed there was some entanglement of which I must be set free. I asked if the change meant success and she said the change itself was a success, but if I meant in the way of fame and fortune (I did), a certain amount of it would come to me

3

though the bulk of recognition would be left for my late years. She told me with precision that I would live to be seventy-eight years old, would have health problems throughout my fifties, and would never be really rich. Like all people who frequent palmists and the like, I took what I wanted to hear and put aside the rest.

The following day Henry Staden's letter arrived telling me of his arrangements. The biggest part of my joy was at leaving Louisville on Derby Day for my week's leave. Louisville is not my favorite city but there are nice things about it; one of these, however, is not Derby Day, a time of appalling avarice on the part of everyone, of German-like public besottedness and misbehavior, and of the exposure of the redneck that apparently lives just beneath the surface in most Southern Ladies and Gentlemen. This revelation generally involves the black servants at house parties. The last time I went to Louisville for a Derby Weekend, in the sixties, it was still going on, this apparent atavism: one party was thrown out of kilter for quite a while because some Lady claimed the black bartender was looking at her with desire.

The day I left, seeing the incoming turmoil at the airport from the calm of my plane which was nearly empty, I said a heartfelt bye-bye and wished it were my final farewell to the town and its people.

The audition acquired me an agent—Audrey Wood, then the top-reigning goddess on that forever-mysterious Olympus of 10-percenters (ah, days of selflessness! Today it's more like 75 percent, I'm told)—and some friends, and a place to stay when I returned. When, indeed. While I was in New York it was announced that all National Guards were to be mobilized. (The other momentous occurrence of that trip was the increase of the cost of a telephone call from a nickel to a dime.)

At the Armory in St. Matthews was a cadre of Regular Army personnel headed by a very G.I. colonel named Shipley, along with the two of us permanent National Guardsmen, Captain Bell and me. Captain Bell told me gloomily that I could not hope for a hearing from Colonel Shipley; he said the man ate, drank, and slept Regulations. Here I was (he said) promised a lucrative theater career (Audrey Wood's letters of promises were being shown proudly around); here I was, a veteran of World War II; and this time, luck being such as it was, I was sure to be killed in Korea after having survived the Japs in Manila. (I did survive, but the war was over when I got there.) Bell himself would probably not survive these later battlefields, and look at him, two babies and a newly mortgaged house. But Shipley (he repeated—there are satisfactions in being a Cassandra and one of these is frequent repetition), Shipley who ate, slept, drank, and excreted Regulations, would not give either one of us a considerate thought.

But what the good captain did not know was that Shipley *read* something other than regulations and one of those things was a book called *The Show Must Go On* by Elmer Rice. This book softened his alleged hard heart and the scrupulously fair man went to Washington and got me unfrozen. It was in September of that same year that I happily left Louisville and the aimlessness of my after-hours circle, bound by alcohol and bitchery, and visited New York again, my second visit. For just one day. Because after that first day I was a New Yorker and have remained one, unshakably, dedicatedly, contentedly. To me this happy state of New Yorkerdom is synonymous with adventure, invitation, license, pleasure, very hard work, pain, and kindness. As I had never been either a Louisvillian or a Kentuckian, by which I mean that there had always been obstacles to my acceptance of either condition, I threw myself like a nearly drowned person into a great hemisphere of air, light, freedom. Louisville had been a closed sphere, escape impossible without the aid of a deus ex machina; New York said to me in accents vulgar and sublime, So live a little. And I began to.

Between the first and second trips I had turned twenty-four, not a bad age at which to draw a first breath. The hell of adolescence was behind me, first serious mistakes had been transcended, I had learned my craft and could make a proper song or an improper one properly; and had just enough living under my belt to know that if I had to go on with what I then had, to the end, the end would be soon.

What dichotomy greater than mine at the time? The macho world of the Armory five and one-half days a week, and two full weeks of bivouac each summer; and every night drag queens and fag mamas and louche bars and bitter fights and the eternal passes thrown by all sexes of all ages at the good-looking country boy. I woke up too many nights to find strange heads bobbing between my legs, for the person I shared my life with was also a voyeur and a locked door was not much protection—one could say that this man's avocation was helping lust laugh at locksmiths.

All that behind me now at age twenty-four. That was my thought as I stepped from my taxi in front of my new temporary home, four doors from Broadway on Forty-third Street. I had been given the room by the friend of a friend. It was to be mine for a week, all of its splintery uncarpeted floor, its bed and chair and bureau, its stained toilet and noisome shower which I could never disinfect of its spermy redolence. But so near home, Broadway!

That night, or early morning, one floor above me a woman

hung from the window bleeding from a cut throat and died there before she could be reached.

I woke to something alien in the room, some familiar thing gone bad. I felt the steel bands within which I could not move and the invasion of what had been me by what had been someone, something. And she screamed again, overhead, and identifying what it was freed me. While I called the police I heard a deep gargling sound like a stream burrowing under rocks. Leaning from the window looking for the help to come I felt something heavy and hot fall on my neck and when I turned face up I saw her and the brilliant blood in the glare of Broadway, and some of her blood fell on my face and a drop of it got in my eye.

I Am Born

I had a quiet taxi driver. As this violated a strict New York precept I decided that he was a New Jerseyan. I flew in to North Field at Newark and was determined to ride into Manhattan in style. Ignoring advice about buses and tubes, I looked for the best vehicle I could find, wishing it could be a limousine, and got in and gave my address and the man clammed up. When I told the story in disbelief to a new acquaintance, in the back of an open limousine driven by a chauffeur later that day, she said it was because of the address. Thus came the introduction to New York's East Side–West Side snobbism. If she said I had been going to any number of good West Side *hotels.* Or to Central Park South. Or Central Park West. Or a number of side streets and a Mews here and a Close there, or somewhere near Columbia University. She advised me: move as quickly as you can to the East Side where a tiny room in the East Seventies wins hands down over an eleven-room apartment somewhere West. I found out that she exaggerated, but not as much as the un-initiate might believe.

I don't know her name though she may have given it when she picked me up. The chauffeur was called Handy and I recall that because it was the name of a character in my musical, a bartender.

I left my untalkative driver and carried my luggage up one flight to the blazing room, dumped it, locked the door, and set off for the City Center. Luise Rainer was acting in *The Lady from the Sea* and I wanted that to be my first New York drama (as opposed to musical; I had seen *Kiss Me, Kate* three times in May, the first three of eleven). I walked up Sixth Avenue so that I might pass Rockefeller Center and enter the Mall and pause above the statue of Prometheus but at Forty-seventh Street I was picked up. I saw the car with the old woman and the old chauffeur driving slowly for the effects of the sun that fell into the canyon. Perhaps I sent a message from a suddenly full heart which was intercepted and caused the following to happen: the car stopped and backed up and tailed into the curb beside me and a voice (not the one the car had summoned for a painful moment) told me to get in. The chauffeur did not open the door but sat stiffly facing forward. I got in. She did not ask where I was going and did not explain why she had stopped. She began to talk and as we drove she pointed out things. How did she know that I did not know what those things were? How had she been able to tell that I was not at that moment a New Yorker? Looking back at that day from here I have the answers. I had and still have a farmer's walk— someone said that even in evening clothes I seem to be stepping over rows of things, or logs. And there were my clothes, plainly stamped Out of Town: the wide-shouldered tan cashmere jacket, the lightweight flannels, the pair of outrageous shoes called Boxcars which, if ever worn in New York, had been worn in the early forties with zoot suits. I never throw anything away and would have the shoes still if they had not caught fire and been damaged beyond wearability (spilled lighter fluid, dropped match, no injury to me). The subtleties of Out of Town engage me now; I live beside the Guggenheim and often watch from our terrace the parade and fancy that I can spot the foreigners and even name their countries—who's to dispute me? In this regrettable day of ubiquitous blue jeans I see the Kansan within the denim.

One extenuating circumstance of anywhere-anytime for me is that I always have to pee. Meetings with strangers exacerbate this proclivity, anticipation of trips does, the hint of any change will. It is a very canine response. And so I rode doggedly in the lovely open car with the talkative lady and grew myself steadily more withdrawn and seemingly morose as desperation spread from the agonized bladder into the brain. When she instructed the chauffeur to take us to Riverside Drive (we were then going up Fifth) I believed that soon despair and urine would mingle unfiguratively. Once on that Drive the lady and I linked arms and she strolled and I hobbled while the car followed our petty pace. I kept darting glances at the slopes falling to the river and the exquisite bushes there, the aegis of cunning little trees, all the natural pissoirs, like a glimpse of paradise denied me. As she spoke and questioned I grunted and plotted, but knew if I whipped it out to frighten her away someone would see me besides Miss Muffet, and I could not (cannot) pee when anyone is watching me. If I am ever hanged I will not void my sins as meant to do, not while the hangman's looking. I crouched beside her more and more ferile and finally the disgusting-ness of it got to her and she asked me abruptly where I had been headed and I told her and they drove me there. We did not speak from Riverside Drive all the way to Fifty-fifth Street where they put me out and I took relief in a subway toilet on a platform pointing the trains in the wrong direction.

As I discovered at 125th Street. But I went up and into Harlem and the familiarity of all the things there and felt at home. I lunched on field peas and fried chicken and sweet potatoes, greens and biscuits. Nobody said, Who, Why, What? nor would they until after the riots of '64. When I finally had my own apartment in Gramercy Park, two years from the time I have now placed us in, when I could not sleep I would take the Third Avenue El to Harlem and wander, my homesickness only for Negroes (as one still said then). After the riots I came to understand that my privilege of going to Harlem in the middle of the night and wandering uncontested was not the privilege of black Harlemites; at that time, found wandering around Gramercy Park, they would be at the least picked up for questioning. And where black rights are concerned, the least (being the most) is seldom forthcoming.

But that day as a tourist, my first day in New York, I experienced the pain of birth and baptism. I arrived having to pee, was treated to the adventure of the strange world and the inevitability of an increasingly cold Mama, felt homesickness, found relief among blacks, and just post-midnight, into my second day, I was baptized by the blood of a sacrificed creature and have kept that spot of blood in my eye. I learned to expect adventure but to maintain disinterestedness, in case; I learned that the odor of sex, unlike the odor of sanctity, cannot be washed from human artifacts.

Within a week I was living on the East Side, about as far east as you can go, just opposite Gracie Mansion on East End Avenue. I was one of what were called "Minnie's People." That was Minnie Astor, who owned the block, or blocks, and took a proprietary interest in us. I lived in a five-room railroad flat furnished with many gifts from Mrs. Astor—sofa, brocade curtains, a pair of Chippendale chairs and the like, for I shared the apartment with a nephew of the Cushing girls, Ben Crowell. In the way of the city I had come circling back to the scene of my first New York triumph, for where I now lived was where I had played my first audition in May 1950.

Impressions and Audition

The day I left Louisville, the first Saturday in May 1950, was oppressively humid. By nine in the morning my clothes clung wetly, the light cotton shorts and shirt I had put on when I got up, grabbing what I could find to cover myself while I negotiated a path through sleeping bodies. They were everywhere available and some places not generally thought to be available, such as the floor of the shower. Louisville is a hospitable place at all times but on Derby Day every door, including those to the most secret closets, is flung open to visitors, or should I say on Derby Eve and earlier, whenever the people begin piling in. Planes, trains, buses are met and the homeless gathered in by not always, I'm afraid, altruistic harvesters. By midnight, Derby Eve, in most houses privacy is a space the mind creates for itself out of necessity. In my bathroom someone was curled around the base of the commode, drunken cheek pressed to the porcelain for its coolness. There was no waking her—a sizable woman, it was, spilling generously out of her bra and what appeared to be a split corset—and I made my ablutions as quietly as I could (euphemism, go home), flushing several times for the pleasure the cold rush undoubtedly brought into the dreams of the sleeping figure, for with each effluence from the tank she stirred and made cooing sounds. Avoiding stepping on her feet, which looked swollen, far too large to fit back into the spectator pumps kicked askew on the floor, I shaved. Because of the figure in the shower, who would surely drown if I abluted over *him,* I made my bath in the basin. I knew that the other bathrooms were officially bedrooms, for the tubs had been outfitted with beach mattresses and pillows.

I suddenly wanted to leave them all as they were and go without the planned escort to the airport. I could envisage the shrill scene at Logan, the shakers of juleps, the general misbehavior.

Afterwards, when I thought of my stealthy departure it was as if I had left a charnel house.

My flight was at noon. I took one of the cars, an old Mercury convertible which I usually drove, and slowly and with intense happiness toured the parks of Louisville, Iroquois and Cherokee. As always I found awesome the oceans of dogwood and redbud undulating in full bloom below when I was on a precipice, and the way, when one drove beneath, they gave the effect of a sunset caught in a canopy. Ireland may be greener than the parks of Louisville but I doubt it—flower-starred greenswards rolling outward to distant rims of forest, great billowing treeshapes like balloons, old willows narcissistic beside far water. And the odor, the overpowering perfume of a wilderness in spring! for Louisville's parks, superbly cared for, are still essentially primeval; as far as I know, no Olmstead has tampered, however brilliantly, with the scenes upon which Daniel Boone had gazed, which before him had sheltered the Indians for whom they were named. The parks were no different from the true wilderness in which I was born and grew and flourished, and from which I yearned to escape as I was now escaping.

I told myself that I was only going to New York to play an audition, if that, for what did I know of the man who had, or said he had, arranged it? Only that he was a book salesman for a big New York publishing house and was said to have connections. He had been brought to my house by people one acquaintance referred to as "our innalecshuls," an unlikely couple composed of a lesbian and an eyebrow-plucking queen, but withal, decent sponsors. And I would be staying with a titular "cousin," a man with whom I shared a surname but as far as we could tell no blood relations.

And yet I felt as though I were bidding Louisville farewell; and in fact when I left again in September it was hurriedly, there *was* a noisy send-off at the airport, and I was drunk. So that lovely quiet drive that Derby Day was my real good-bye to a place where I had been miserable more than happy, but which I found physically beautiful. Louisville, like the Îles of Paris, is made up of courts, squares, little and big parks, gardens, mews. In flowering seasons the smell of blossoms can (could) overwhelm the breweries in the west end— themselves giving off a not unpleasant odor and to drinkers and lovers of fresh bread a highly enjoyable one.

Driving from Iroquois to Cherokee I went down South Third Street and past my first home in Louisville, a classical house that had been turned into an inn. Before I went to Louisville, fresh out of World War II, I read the ad in a newspaper and determined to live there. It turned out to be too expensive for me in the long run but I scraped along for a couple of months in the charming place. There was a cultured concierge, as she preferred to be called, and quite wonderful rooms; separate tables for dining and a resident countess. This was an American woman who had married a Russian count. She was then of that age best called indeterminate; she was genteelly poor and kept her handsome old Packard and chauffeur by lunching only once a week in the best place, otherwise never going out, and she contrived that I should never see her other than by candlelight. Cynical fellow-boarders hinted that she was in love with me, which flattered me but otherwise did no good. She and I discussed Scarlatti (about whom I knew absolutely nothing), books (on which I was better informed), and she taught me some things about food preparation, such as the discreet use of nutmeg where others would fling in a handful of pepper. On my twentieth birthday she prepared, in a chafing dish at a table for the two of us set in the drawing room away from the cynics, my first really exquisite meal. It was lobster Newburg and nothing since has been as perfect as that first exposure to lobster in a sauce of Madeira, cream, egg yolks, cognac. I see her, my first countess, by candlelight, the little silver dishes of ingredients ornamental around the glimmer of the chafing dish, handling so delicately the silver tools of cookery; the lace of her blouse encloses her throat and around the lace are pearls; her auburn hair is loosely swept up and looks soft, tendrilly, in its vague cushion shape; on her hands, as always, are mitts which leave only the fingers exposed, and this night of my birthday the mitts are of the same stiff-looking lace as her choker collar; her skirt is long with a dull sheen, the color of the champagne (sham*pine,* she pronounced it) in our tall, thin glasses. Cooking the marvelous food she tells me that what she is doing is very fin de siècle. Years later, writing songs for my second countess, I wrote one, cruel in its Midwestern mispronunciations, called "Fin de Sickle" ("Dickies and jabots will be lacy / Underwear is pos'tively racy / Pretty soon we'll be in a pickle / Watch your step, it's fin de sickle"). And I thought of her, her careful French, the discretion with which she spoke and moved, the care she took to conceal her age, and longed to know her again, to have the chance to take full advantage of her, of what she so diffidently offered, which was—among *other things,* according to my cynical acquaintants at the Red Door Inn—to teach me. For I had eschewed college, suffering the equivalent of what an Indian friend later wrote about in the plight of young Indians home from school, called England-returned. I was war-returned and restless, and we were legion; but I at least knew that enrolling at that time in a university would be a futile thing, a waste of the G.I. Bill. But there in memory sits my university, who wanted in return, I think, only the tuition of my young-ness. There was no real flirtation, no innuendo, as between Ella and Gareth in *The Tattooed Countess.* She was as sexless as a beautiful formal portrait.

Two painful memories enclose her icon (the candlelit room, the glowing silver and pearls, her erect head with cameo profile). The first memory is of overhearing her talk-ing to the concierge, raging, really, about the humiliation of having been offered a seat on a city bus by someone older than she was: *Older than I!*—her vehemence, her vituperative disbelief; part of that memory is of having to accept the idea of her riding like ordinary people on city buses and streetcars. The second memory is of the one time I saw her in sunlight, the way she tried to shield her face from me by pretending to have left something in the Packard and burrowing back into its shadows. She said to me, "You go on in, don't wait," and then angrily, *"Do not wait."* The old chauffeur stood impas-sively holding the door. (When I saw the open limousine on

Sixth Avenue the thought that put a lump in my throat was of my countess having the courage of sunlight.) On her public luncheon days I had always been at my job (*a* job; I was then on my second or third, the famous restlessness and inefficiency of the war-returned), but on this day I had been fired. My sheaf of lyrics typed on company time on company paper had been found in the drawer of my desk. This meant, I knew, that I could not stay at the inn beyond my paid-up week—it was a Wednesday—and it seems fitting if terrible that I should have seen her and thus lost her and my job on the same day. But she would not face me again and after my second attempt I did not try anymore.

It was too warm on that day for her choker collar or fur neckpieces. The concealing arabesques of the heavy veiling that fell below her chin were inadequate to the ruthless sunlight of South Third Street at 2:00 p.m. and she could not forgive me. If I had told her that I grew up among the old, that wrinkles were as familiar to me as smooth skin, that wrinkled and smooth were only alternate ways of appearing, it would probably have horrified and enraged her. Quite some time later I ran into Mrs. Westbrook, our concierge, in a department store and could tell that she wanted to impart something to me that might be indiscreet; finally she flung indirection impatiently away and told me the method whereby the countess handled unhappiness was to sleep and that following (the whole inn knew about it) our encounter in the sunlight she had slept for four days. Mrs. Westbrook said it was more like a coma, for she could not be wakened, that pulse and respiration dropped to the bare-discernible, and that during these trances it was essential for a doctor to check her at least once a day—that the countess had given these instructions to her soon after moving in. Mrs. Westbrook was

apologetic—didn't I see that the countess had not been
denying me? For her part, she was so sorry not to have told
me at the time. Turning to leave she turned back and rather
shyly revealed the deep, unsuspected romantic, "She wears
it, you know. Always." Once the countess had asked me
where I got the little gold pen I wore as a tieclasp and I told
her on the spur of the moment, thinking it would somehow
make me glamorous and dangerous, that I had stolen it. She
had not believed me and tapped my hand reprovingly with a
long fingernail. The day of my departure I left with the
concierge to be given to my countess the pen with a note
saying, in the language she would have taught me, "C'est
vrai."

I recall that my revery in front of the inn was broken by the
appearance of four jockeys abreast, tiny swaggering bow-
legged figures in full racing kit, set now against the glare of a
mean-intentioned sun (the temperature that May day reached
into the nineties; I read about it in cool New York). This told
me that time had moved apace (as my grandparents actually
said) and I whizzed through Cherokee, above which I could
see on its hill the rather imposing house in which I lived, then
returned the car to the six-car garage which itself sat on
higher ground above the house and walked up to Bardstown
Road and caught a taxi.

Looking down toward the house from the garage, I had
seen in none of the windows a shadow of a moving creature,
though in the kitchen the cook probably moved around cut-
ting country ham, setting out grits, breaking eggs, fetching fig
jam from the pantry, sifting ingredients for biscuits, making
coffee—all in large quantity for I was sure that as many as
thirty people were domiciled in the mock-Elizabethan pile.
Somewhere behind the crossed timbers and stucco was the

man I was leaving, busy at frosting mugs and crushing mint
and ice, aided by his black butler-chauffeur who went everywhere with him, with us, as did three of the maids. (Later
they were to back a van up to the house when no one was
there and take a great many valuables, many of which they
were allowed to keep in return for silence.) No one in the
house yet knew that I had gone. Every thought of mine that
penetrated behind that facade below presented itself to me
as too rich: the food heavy on ham fat and butter, the smooth
old bourbon a minimum of twenty-one years in the cask, the
scents of Vetiver and Woodhue and Aphrodisia, the accents
of the speech—jocular, hyperbolic, with emphases made in
Country: "I'm jis a ol cuntry boy m'sef and this hi 'ciety's too
rich fu m'BLOOD." I saw the crossed timbers as bars.

The pre-jet flight took just under three hours; it was called a
Constellation Flight, the best the country then offered, and it
was as if my desire were pushing the plane.

New York. So beautiful from the air, so liberating on the
ground. After Louisville it was cool, almost chilly, in the low
sixties, and there was an effervescence that was (is) like no
other place. Of all polluted cities New York has retained
more of its purity, or has kept the arcane ability to recapture it
for stretches of time when the high breezy sky might play
host again to carrier pigeons; perhaps this is because of its
situation amid rivers and bays and seas, which act as filters,
drawing in the foul exudations of the Gulf and the Midwest
and sieving it, giving the city back the cleaned air and
spitting the worst parts far out to sea. In 1950 one did not
hear the word *pollution* and the cleanness was not so illusory.
But still, when all things conspire today, in the 1980s, there is
the winey air which conduces to twilights like the offspring

of an amethyst and a ruby, and to the fabulous clarity which erases distance. (From my study window now there is no north; the cityscape ends short of 110th Street; but tonight, or tomorrow morning or night, George Washington Bridge will seem to be on the next block, and to the south there will be the cleanly etched buildings that edge the Park, each window boldly drawn, and the Central Park West towers will show bronze in a long lingering sunset, and above them will be the planes flickering silver upon a night sky of Arabian blue, royal blue, charcoal purple.)

That first day I naturally noticed the dirty streets, a sight never seen in Louisville, streets strewn with garbage and above all with newspapers—the streets paved not with gold but with news. And I was not revolted but felt strangely cozy. I went to my cousin's office to fetch the key and then by cab to the Village (Edna St. Vincent Millay lightly on my mind— her narrow house) and to the garden within which stood the carriage house my cousin was lucky enough to inhabit. One got to the garden through the hallway of the apartment building in front, then crossed its little rather scruffy places which could have borne a paradise, then into the enchanting house of three floors, all of them indescribably filthy. It was as though I had brought the New York streets with me like a new scroungy lover and again I did not mind—this was the way people lived in New York. I was so in love that if there had been *merdes* on the floor I would not have objected. Happily my cousin's sense of hygiene stopped short just this side of that.

In the evening Walter took me to Times Square. That is another first never to be duplicated: the shock of that alien glare can be felt only once. And the noise and the sleazy shops of "final sales" with their windows full of "original oil

21

paintings" and unspeakably touching objets d'art. The clumps of freakish people gathered on corners were like vampires there in their greeny skins for a convention, contrasted to the theatergoers, the majority of them out-of-towners like me, the women in pastel colors and pale fur the deadliest give-away. The big splashy restaurants, most of them gone today, seemed to define Broadway and Seventh Avenue. We ate that night at Toffenetti's and saw the Keene Sisters on their way to play the Copa. My attention was drawn to the Adelphi Theatre because of my constant search for auguries and because of its name redolent of oracles. Out loud I said my name as though reading it on the marquee in high letters like those advertising the appearance of the Divine Sarah (Vaughan) and Lady Day, competing Goddesses of the Street. In less than a year it was indeed there, briefly, and on that day as I gazed at it time compressed. It was as if Louisville were superimposed over New York, Derby Day above the shove and clamor of Broadway, and around it all lay the shadow of the future which I could discern but could not trace with eager eyes, nor from its smoke could I define a readable shape. These things happen when you see your name in lights for the first time, even though the occasion is just a television show for which you have composed the songs. I thought it might be like a living person looking at the grave-stone upon which his name has been carved with his date of birth, only the day of his death missing—but it is there in smoke. . . . I stood with Elaine Stritch once watching the letters of her name go up one at a time. She was breathless with melancholy. . . . Before the television show had sung its heart out and Lee Wiley had made her "comeback" from what some said had been a ten-year drunk, workmen were dismantling the marquee of its legend. When I came out into

the night two syllables were left of my name: **man**   well.
Years later in the process of denigrating a show of mine,
Miss Judith Crist addressed in print her mentor, asking "Get
the picture, Manny?" and I thought of that marquee and
man   well.

Walter and I finished the night's roaming (for love itself
must rest) in the silent deeps of Wall Street, an experience
that cannot be successfully described, not in words, not by
me. I can't write poetry, which might serve; and am incapable
of writing the kind of music that could approximate it. I
remember though how the late-rising moon lay between,
upon, the buildings as if seeking a reflection in dark water far
below, for such is the semblance of night within the banks of
Wall Street. The moon's light was given back to her in thousands of fragments—of metal, glass, silence; of long cistern-
like echoes. This was like a melancholic ecstasy, like the end
of love; but maybe I think that because I once ended a love
affair in those ravines and can hear his crying still. I did not
make a sound; I was afraid of leaving my chagrin there for
someone to hear on another such night. I think now that that
first night with Walter I believed I could hear weeping in the
wind as it hung at corners; I know we discussed the way it
seemed to loiter there as though peering down the dark lanes
before furtively moving on. It is a very dramatic way to end
one's first night in New York, or one's fifth or sixth love affair.

Waiting for the audition, feeling less assured of my worth
with each day's passing, I did idle New York things with the
dedication of an ill-at-ease provincial. I lay in the fountain in
Washington Square, dry I assume on account of the dreadful
drought; I wandered along the Hudson as far up as Grant's
Tomb; I frequented Village bars too early in the day, and
boasted too late into the night to strangers of the glittering

career ahead of me. The boasts grew broader as my prospects mentally narrowed. I had sex with anybody who wanted to, of whatever sex, color, or condition. I lay in the dirt of a basement entranceway with a one-legged black man. I fucked a stone-deaf girl who was also missing her left arm from the elbow down. She was, understandably, the most bitter person I've ever met and I think it was more because of the deafness than the mutilation. A deaf person must fight paranoia at every turning, fight the belief that the words of others are deliberately muffled. This girl, Cara, was very pretty in a 1920s way, a cloche of polished black hair, boy's figure, translucent skin, a cape to mask the missing arm. I met her as part of a couple in a bar but she was open about wanting sex with me and she had a place to go and so we went, walking from Eighth Street to Seventeenth where she was domiciled in a cheerless room. Afterward, back in the bar, she introduced the boy we had left as her husband. It was he who told me that they were on their honeymoon. I wonder if he has killed her or divorced her, for she pled with each cruel word and action for some final gesture. Sleeping with her was like being entangled in a thorn thicket or a roll of barbed wire. She was spiky, vicious, and rather low. When I was tardy she told me sneeringly to "Git it ühp" and that ühp was like a strange thing which lived under her tongue. She wanted to be slapped in the face and when I found this hard to do, she saw to it that it became easier, until at last it was a kind of pleasure, or relief. Learning the game, I baited her by pretending to speak words that she could not lip-read, because they were not words at all but made-up shapes for my mouth and her paranoia. She was so enraged by this that she screamed, the screams toneless like the sounds a rock might make. Which, I suppose, is pretty close to what a deaf head must feel like.

I saw to it that she came, I had my pride, and years later found my experience unpleasantly set forth in a famous story, including the method by which I induced her release.

In the unfortunate way of things, that sexual experience has stayed with me while many others of intense pleasure involving feelings of love are wrapped closely and tucked deeply away and must be dug for. Is it human nature thus defined, or only my own? I know that hatred is stronger than many varieties of love, which has as many varieties as flowers; and that hateful sex, being traumatic, etches itself upon the first available surface, a decidedly un-Freudian theory. But I've found on going back to my past in little dips like a bird hopping around a birdbath and sipping, it is the sweetness of some of the water that surprises me. I expect the filth, the droppings, which I can plainly see on the bottom, for I have looked at it nightly sometimes for weeks at a stretch, for thirty-five years and longer.

The Wednesday of the audition comes, a day of low clouds and small flurries of rain, promising to the drought-stricken city. I don't recall one event of the day before my arrival at Ben Crowell's on East End Avenue at 4:30. Cousin Walter goes with me. The apartment is pleasant, though dark, with handsome furniture and beautiful flowers. The piano is a spinet, which Mr. Crowell says he has had tuned for me. He offers us a drink which I decline, saying I will make up for it after the audition. But as the guests arrive and I am introduced I begin to make little trips back to the bar which is set up in the second room of a long sequence; for if I have not heard of the people, Cousin Walter has, and I am afraid his emphases upon *who* they are is not meant to soothe me. Here are Ivan Obolensky and his wife Claire; David McDowell and

25

his wife, Madeline, an Italian marquesa (I am quickly told by Walter) whom they call Poopie; here are other names I have read in columns in the past few days and here is Tennessee Williams. He seems not to know where he is nor why he is here. Inquiring about a painting, which is by Emanuel Romano, he asks Ben Crowell to have Romano paint him "one like it." But I do not care what he says or how he looks (vague, troubled, spaced-out) for I had seen *A Streetcar Named Desire* in Louisville a short time before and had not been able to get up from my seat until the auditorium was emptied. This certainly calls for another drink. Soon I am not quite leaving the room with the bar but am lingering in the doorway with the sense of spying and eavesdropping. Several times Ben Crowell tries to draw me into a group but is deterred, I think, by what must have been a growing wildness about me. I recall a feeling of ruthless despair at the meagerness of the talent soon to be displayed, or exposed. Once I am afflicted by dry heaves and stand in the bathroom shuddering over the commode, feeling homesick, not for Louisville and its perfidy (they said I had talent!) but for the wilderness and Mama. I stand by the open bathroom window bathed in the rainy air and think I can hear Mama singing beyond the door, high and reedy, "Brighten the Corner Where You Are." Behind my closed lids the bathroom assumes the shape of the chimerical one at home in which I performed my first songs because of the remarkable effects given to music by the three-story height of the cylinder containing the commode and high-hung tank with its long chain; this wild fantasy of a room (a slightly enlarged dumbwaiter shaft), down which wind howled and birds fell, was my first recording studio, or the shaft of the first spotlight within which I stood, the youngest Star in the world.

With closed eyes I leave the Crowell bathroom carrying with me the images and ambitions and beliefs fostered in the other, and without preamble I go to the piano and begin my audition, freed back into the condition of performer.

After the second song Williams sits forward and praises what he has heard, inquiring who has written such a ravishing work of art. (During the opening, a Chorus for Whores, he had sat as though stunned.) He still does not know where or why or who. But, Work of Art! Wait, I promise him in my head, and play my heart out, caterwauling theatrically on the songs meant to be showstoppers. One, called "Try Me," does indeed bring down the house, helped by my audience's familiarity by this time with the prudish social worker whose number it is; the character is drunk and I am drunk and the result is funny and sexy. Years later when I play the song for Lena Horne ("Try me / for size then buy me / if I fit / Test me / then love, love-nest me / if I'm it") she says, "My God, they think I make 'Honeysuckle Rose' dirty! I just never could get away with it."

The audition is a genuine success. The story of the musical, which involves a love affair between a white woman and a black man whose baby she is about to have at final curtain, is pronounced remarkably daring (and it was, and was never done because of that); the music is compared to Kurt Weill crossed with Puccini, not too difficult an assessment as my opening Chorus for Whores was based (deliberately) on "Vissi d'arte," and I was under the influence at that time of the Weill of *Love Life* and *One Touch of Venus*. These were not bad models, and the songs were my own, not copies.

I am heady with victory and drink and Williams asks me to go with him into another room where we can talk. Walter's eyes follow and so, I discover in a moment, does Walter.

Williams and I settle onto a Directoire couch in the room with the whiskey, from which neither of us keeps a distance, and there we talk, or rather, there I answer questions. When he asks where I was born, saying he can discern but not identify a slight accent, I tell him without hesitation, Cairo, Egypt. I am a bit surprised, for I have never been attracted to Egypt. But Cousin Walter is so astounded that he steps out of his sentry post behind the doorjamb to say, "You were *not*. You *may* have been born in Cairo, *Kentucky*." (I was not.) And I disown him, telling Williams in cold earnestness that I have no idea who that old man is (Walter Dowell was then in his upper forties). And I leave with Williams and a very odd little man with a twisted face named Paul Bigelow. We go to Williams's suite in the Sherry Netherland where I without any further ado pass out.

I came to in a bathtub empty of water though there were cold compresses on my head and other pulse points. And between my legs—an acrobatic feat in itself—bobbed the familiar-unfamiliar head. It was not Williams's head; I was no longer at the hotel but in another railroad flat down the block from the scene of my symbolic death and rebirth. What I was undergoing was meant I suppose as a kind of religious ritual too, for the doer gasped between takes, "Por Dios, por Dios." And I joined in, intoning from Williams's play, "Flores, flores para los muertos."

Afterward over coffee I was informed that Williams was much taken with me and wished me to "wait upon him" at his hotel the next evening at 11:30 to which he would return from dining at Mona Williams's (no relation). I went as much because of the courtly locution of the invitation as for any other reason. He was fairly prompt and I was expected and

Bigelow showed up with a very handsome boy, a young painter, clearly meant for Williams's delectation. But there was no taking. I stayed with Tennessee that night and the remaining two nights of my stay in New York. I was flying back on Sunday afternoon.

There was little sexual behavior between us, and no sensuality. What occurred was anti-hot, like taking a sip of water from the carafe in the small hours and finding it tepid and a bit metallic. But what we shared is to me more interesting than repetitions of awkward sex could have been. While Bessie Smith sang the same songs over and over on the portable phonograph, Williams lay, on bed or sofa, and talked of his fears and frustrations. Earlier he would have laughed telling us how he had been insulted at dinner—a woman saying to him "What on earth are *you* doing here?" and objecting to his mustache; telling how he had invited her to clip it for him, he had chuckled with seemingly real amusement. But in the bluesy dim ambiance of Bessie Smith his fear of such women would be aired; and his fear of success, of being abandoned, of losing Frankie (his lover, visiting family in New Jersey), of going to pot, would be released into the custody of his young psychiatrist and Williams would feel better. It was then that some sort of sexual thing might occur. But I felt worse and worse; by the end of our third night together I felt drained and incredibly looked forward to going back to Louisville. I think his fears for himself caused my own for myself to surface; never too deeply buried, they were drawn up like earthworms by rain through this lionized man's unrest, through his inability to accept and revel in what he must have been working for, for many years, and dreaming of while he washed greasy dishes by the kitchenful.

29

When I returned in September I called Williams as he had asked me to do. And he could not remember me. I protested, "But I stayed with you for three nights!" The silence on the telephone was equivalent to an ironic shrug, albeit an apologetic one. Over the years I would see him at parties around New York and he would always look haunted, asking where we had met, but I never told him. Once he asked me to join a clothes club to which he belonged, the tiny Mr. Bigelow among the members. They simply pooled their clothes and wore them interchangeably. I was well over six feet tall and wondered how they thought they would manage with my clothes, or I with theirs. That was the strangest membership I have ever been offered. Williams had asked about my suit, a handsome, scratchy shetland which in cold weather would lacerate my legs to the knee, and I had told him (that day's version of Cairo, Egypt) that it was made from the hair of my childhood pony which had died only a year before at some astronomical age. So I imagined it was not the suit itself but the fame of the suit that he wanted.

Years went by and I did not encounter him again, our circles having become unalterably de-homogenized. In 1976 he gave a testimonial for a novel of mine; James Laughlin had asked him to read it. He invoked his most sacred icon, Jane Bowles, to describe what he felt to be my achievement in the book, *Island People.* Friends have said, "But you know him, don't you?" And I have truthfully answered, "No." For there was no line running from the fifty-year-old novelist back to the young songwriter-psychiatrist, and the assumption of my friends that a bit of noblesse oblige was involved in the encomium printed on the jacket of my novel is erroneous. The praise had to be given purely for one reason: he would have had no idea of who I was.

Somewhere in the midst of my last few days in New York I called Ben Crowell to thank him for his kindness, to hear about the arrival of my flowers, and unexpectedly to receive an invitation to stay with him when I came back. For he, and the rest of them, he said, were all convinced that I would be back, Korea notwithstanding; Audrey Wood, he said, to whom I had been recommended by Williams and Bigelow (she was Williams's agent), had taken me on and according to Crowell, Korea was no match for Audrey.

Word had filtered to Louisville of what happened in New York and I returned to a decidedly mixed press: most people were impatient even before they heard my recountals and soon enough I found myself without an audience.

I kept to myself and the man in whose house I continued to live and I drifted apart—like, I thought, rudderless craft on separate currents; but by the time I left he was involved with someone else and came to New York only twice, driving in a station wagon to bring me some furniture. A very nice gesture.

Within a couple of months, for the first time in my life, I was free, without ties or obligations to another person. (One is tied to family, then to classmates, then to school, or army, after which one is entitled to first freedom. I had foregone that freedom by forming the early neurotic attachment, very much like unfinished business with my father.) So when I say that I was born at age twenty-four, it will be understood what I mean.

Crowell was away that first week when I arrived in September; I had been informed by letter that he would be, so that I had time, in the frightful apartment on Forty-third Street, to build up a terrific wish for civilized living again. No Gypsy I, then or now; like Marc Blitzstein's Regina, I'm in love with things.

31

Crowell was a nephew of the (famous) Cushing girls of Boston, who had become Mrs. Vincent Astor, Mrs. Jock Whitney, and Mrs. William Paley—respectively, not in succession. I met all of them a number of times and made no impression and surprisingly received very little. This may be because I am not a camera but something more on the order of litmus paper, and perhaps those three nice ladies did not have enough acid base to register deeply. I recall one of them had a charming kind of slang—"worn to a frazz"—but can't remember which one. I think Mrs. Paley was the real beauty though I remember them all as very fine, and definitely recollect (that sweet old word) Minnie Astor's long legs. To her sisters I imagine I was just one of Minnie's odd people and to her I was one of Ben's odd friends.

I was often asked to parties and weekends by people I met through Ben, people with large houses above the Hudson or on (as I came to call it) the North Sore, and learned after a sample or two to decline. I did not play bridge, my tennis game was competent but unexciting, and I did not like having to rent a dinner jacket, for I could not maintain one permanently in the manner to which it was accustomed. (A nostalgic note is that a decent one could be bought then at Brooks or J. Press for ninety dollars.)

One weekend to which I did go featured, I suppose that's the word, the Duke and Duchess of Windsor. Crowell went too and he and I compared notes and stories. He was in his element; I did not then have an element and so drifted somewhat ghostily; in a little room one late night someone referred to me with affection as "the boy across the room." Ben was amused by almost everything in life but not by the Windsors. Jimmy Donahue was there also, being in the midst of his Duchess phase, or she in her Donahue phase; in any case he was there and another reason I was sorry not to have stayed at home. I found him one of the most terrifying people I had (have) ever met. There was an aura about him of things unspeakable, I imagine like that which enclosed Aleister Crowley; his pretty-boy face seemed like a mockery. People did speak of certain of his escapades, such as his having stripped someone naked in the winter and tied him to a tree in Central Park where he remained in subfreezing weather all night. There was a lawsuit; the victim was "fixed" for life from Donahue's pocket; and I imagine, maimed in some way, also for life.

Crowell found the Windsors silly in one instance and dull in the other (I forget which was which). I formed no opinion but observed that her clothes were beautiful and her skin so clean-looking that one imagined the pores had been reamed; her hair shone and her eyes were bitter. One game of hers: after a meal one evening she went round the circle of women pointing out whose jewels were real and whose paste. "Your emeralds are paste," and the startled woman admitted that the real ones were in the vault. And so on until the Duchess came to some apparently superb diamonds upon which she said, "I've always wanted diamonds," and the old boy said in his cockney accent, "You can't have everything, my dear."

This seemed to me terribly moving. I had been twelve years old when I heard in the bosom of my family the speech of abdication. There had been some rancorous comments by my father about what women can cause men to do for them. My mother, an optimist, said soothingly that love was stronger than anything and was not to be deplored. (She wasn't romantic at all but wanted I imagine to implant in us a positive feeling about that most romantic of twentieth-century events.) Anyway, I told Crowell just how moved I was and he laughed at my naïveté, saying that Windsor had given up a throne he both feared and detested, that he would have been the worst possible thing for England because his boredom threshold was so low; if forced to be king he would have, out of boredom, done things infinitely worse than abdication, such as collaboration with Germany in the war, toward which he tended naturally anyhow on account of blood and stupidity. He put a cap on the Windsors by quoting Donahue on his reason for being seen so often in the company of the Duchess. Donahue had said, "For the same reason that the old boy abdicated: because she sucks a better cock than any man I know."

Crowell, a seemingly reformed alcoholic, had, in his last bout with the disease, nearly burned himself to death and his body, as I was to discover, was a mass of scars and rubber-like welts. Because of his proclivity, his father, a Cleveland jeweler, cut him off without a cent but his mother provided for him under imposed conditions which included surveillance, so that her provision could be taken away at any serious infraction of the rules.

When I last saw Crowell he was living in Oaxaca with a heterosexual young Mexican for a lover, and employed the best cook in town. They lived in a handsome walled house where Ben spent his time learning about Oaxaca and Mexico, especially her ruins, especially Monte Albán. But his reason for being in that country was not an earnest interest in things Mexican but rather because he had scarcely any money left and could only afford the quieter town and not the more expensive San Miguel de Allende where several of his friends had settled for reasons similar to his. He told us that the house and cook cost him fifty dollars a month. I don't know if the young lover had a price beyond that of the automobile Ben gave him; if the boy's freedom was costly to Ben he did not say so.

The only bitterness I ever heard out of Crowell's mouth was his expression of puzzled dislike for his dead father, voiced over tequila in a café on the Zócolo, for he was drinking again. A year or so after I was in Oaxaca word came of his death from drink-related causes. Crowell's humane potential was much greater than that of most people I have met who were born into riches. I have often wondered since his death what it might have been like for him, and others who cared for him, if his father had shared some of the guilt for Ben's alcoholism.

Crowell was the first of two people I have met who suffered similar fates because of cruel fathers and kind mothers. The second was an English ladyship whose father, an earl, had cut her off without a penny, which seems tiresomely to be the first thought and impulse of men in a certain financial stratum as soon as their children display independence. Lady L's failing was not alcohol but racehorses. In view of the disinheritance one has to assume that she did not in the long run do too well, but all she spoke of in that connection was the £10,000 brought in by one of her loves, a filly. Dear Mum, who was part American, provided for her bereft daughter whose very house was taken from her and given to his mistress by the new earl, her brother. . . .

My friend's bitterness, unlike Crowell's, went everywhere with her and was capable of infecting a populace when she had drunk enough; her tears of shocking reminiscence were dreadful to experience; she was as desolate in her remembrance as anyone or anything, including Lear on his blasted heath. At those times she was as inconsolable as cold clay.

This lady was responsible for the publication of my first novel (*The Grass Dies* in England, *One of the Children Is Crying* here), which had been turned down in America by twenty-four publishers. She gave me her publisher's address in London and recommended me to them with fine British heartiness; two of her novels had made the National Book List and so her word was good. Without this intervention in my life I daresay I would not have had a career even of sorts. I had just about given up hope, was drug addicted, alcoholic, and very nearly a suicide. The diet of dissembling and foolish rejection letters, which seldom approached the matter of the book but listened to their own brain-rattlings of stock phrases, has starved to death, I am convinced, many decent artists before they could begin. This sort of gaucherie, based on formula and fear of the new, is best exemplified in the *Kirkus* notices, which are more like *trous de loup* than legitimate criticism. Obstacles they certainly are, with the book as the enemy. As in the rejection letters (just now one discovers that the Pulitzer novel *Ironweed* received fourteen rejections) there is in one's *Kirkus* response more than a suspicion that the book has not been read; rather, that the "reviewer," for his twenty-five dollar fee, has written a fragment of a novel using one's title, which he or she then proceeds to demolish. In none of my notices, and some have been what I am sure they thought were "good," has there been anything approaching accuracy or disinterestedness. In my last novel, as of this writing (*White on Black on White*), the *Kirkus* version is that the homosexual narrator keeps after a black hit man to go with him to the country until the black man gives in; in the novel it is the black man who persuades the narrator to rent the house. But to have set this down in their notice would have meant to abandon the, as far as I know, pre-prejudice with which the book was to be approached. Prejudice, inattention, a kind of resident viciousness—these deathless qualities in the *Kirkus ton* have led me to the certainty that my reviews have all been written by the same person and to the surreal conclusion that his name is Swan. Or her name; the writing always features a certain macho femininity.

As soon as the novel was bought by England, Random House, which had turned it down once, snapped it up and tried to dictate the British publication date, saying that I was an American author and should be published first in my own country. All at once I was wrapped about with coziness, two publishers and politesse on both sides of the Atlantic, decent advances and editors who "believed" in the book. At Random House there was a second printing; in Britain there were extraordinary reviews; and in America also, marvelous reviews. But none in New York. This killed the book at Random House. Death by omission, death by publisher. This unearthed for me something hidden as deep—well, how deep is the human mind? Do we speak at all of depth and when we do, are we accurate? Tunnels, labyrinths, need not delve, but contain their secrets in elbows, turnings, closets. Whether deep or parallel to the surface like a mole's long house, I had tucked away, with what arcane ritual known only to children I cannot guess, a terror. Here is the way it came nudging up or out, like a tapeworm drawn by the smell of food; here is the way I wrote it down, not knowing what I was writing, in 1968, italics and all. *The child struggles to breathe behind the closet door which fits so tightly into the wainscoting that no outline can be discerned at twilight, the time of incarceration, the hour when they like to work in the cool garden in summer among the vegetables and flowers and the house is empty and filling with shadows like the barrel under the eaves during a rainstorm. But first the pillow to take the breath and then quickly the closet as tight as a coffin. Straining to hear, straining to see, small sips of air to make the supply last. A smell of heavy purple and behind the eyes red going darker. And the air going and beyond the door, threat lies waiting. The screen door spring whines and one second before they come in lighting lights on their way, one second before blackout in the closet, the door is sneakily opened and you stumble out and puke on the rug, all the slime and snot and dark purple dust.*

Before Christmas in 1950 I was appointed staff composer on the DuMont television network, which was Channel 5 and scarcely top echelon. I had a new roommate in Bill Lesley, who was curator at the Cooper Union Museum. He was a splendid, rather foxy-looking fellow, whose idea of happiness was for him to sit in a chair with me on the floor at his feet, my head lightly against his knee, his hand lightly upon my hair, while the vast repertoire of Mozart unfolded around us like dark golden roses. I will always be grateful to Lesley for that early exposure to Mozart, and for the people I met through him, including Lotte Lehmann and Andre Koussevitzky. At the house of people named Schaeffer I was frequently in rooms where the only ornament would be a great Rembrandt or the work of another painter of similar stature. Schaeffer was an art dealer and the paintings hung in his own house while prices were negotiated with museums. Or with Texans, who had just discovered "original oil paintings." As the century moves along the gap between the ridiculous and the sublime closes, led by the Texan victory of money over taste which began to show, like a sheep in a boa constrictor, in the early fifties. It was along about then that Sir

Thomas Beecham, who knew how to butter his bread, called life in Dallas the peak of Western civilization. It was also to Dallas that Wallis Warfield Simpson, Duchess of Windsor, took her used clothes to sell. Valentina, who made many of those clothes, said Her Grace was built like a boa constrictor.

One evening at the Schaeffers', in the shadow of a great painting unveiled for the occasion—I recall turbans, pearls, a kingly type, and a slave, all the shimmer intensified and the details blurred by my myopia—Lotte Lehmann sang to a small party by candlelight. It was Koussevitzky who accompanied her. The next evening I shared an opera box at a moving *Rosenkavalier* (Rose Bampton, Frances Bible) with Kalla Halász, whose husband was then director of the New York City Opera, and with Risë Stevens at the fulltide of her glamour.

After so much taking on faith, one evening I was asked just what it was that I did exactly. I can see Lesley's embarrassed face as I say "Television." He looks on the edge of collapse when I am asked to play something of mine. The kindly (and hilarious) response is that my music shows a healthy Mozartian influence. The piece was a little TV opera for three people, a lawyer and a couple seeking a divorce, and it was pure Mozart, two bars here, a fragment there. But I had not done it deliberately; it had occurred by osmosis during the nightly concerts and only when I played it in that company could I hear what I had done with Lesley's persistent influence.

Thus as usual in my life two worlds marched in parallel columns, worlds as yet unassimilable. These were the worlds of art and grand opera and their mainly German supporters in America, and the newest, brashest form of mass appeal, television. A witticism from each world defines, I think, the distance between. At the Cooper Union a very rich woman's purse was responsible for many of its treasures, but along with it went the woman herself—her taste, her opinions, her dictates. Giving an ultimatum before his resignation, someone, perhaps Lesley (ascriptions of wit are dangerous), said, "I cannot make a silk ear out of a sow's purse." Down in the purlieus of Tin Pan Alley, Reuben's, and the gutted and remodeled Adelphi Theatre, a man named Fink had taken to reviewing the TV shows, invariably lofty and dismissive of actors, material, and medium. One week the typesetter played this Fink into our hands by printing his byline as *Fick*. And people went around saying, "Funk you, Mr. Fick."

My weekly show required a minimum of two songs and sometimes as many as ten, which meant that I would write them in the bathroom after Lesley had gone to sleep. I had tried slipping out to walk along the East River, that lovely parapet, windy and deserted, from Eighty-third Street to Ninetieth, but Lesley slept too lightly and woke several times a night to check on me. He said that I flapping along the river in my cape was begging to be raped or worse. And so I wrote my tunes silently, four rooms from him, and went to rehearsals often without any sleep at all. Such seeds planted deep and young will bear a harvest. Mine was—but not for awhile yet— a nervous breakdown, a term still then in use.

My songs were sung by Elaine Stritch, a Broadway show-stopper ("Bongo Bongo Bongo") who became my best friend; Charlotte Rae, so funny on camera and so somber off; and Beatrice Arthur—I think she burped one of my songs; she made her professional debut on our show. To my immense satisfaction now and then an opera singer would venture onto the little screen on our show and the Geminian dichotomy of my life would be suddenly healed like the closing of a wound

41

and I would take this triumph home to Lesley, who was never impressed. Broadway, the goal of my ambition, was bad enough; but television? He watched from the control booth one show of mine and blushed painfully all the way through it. When I huffily said, "I didn't tell you to expect Gluck," he said, "No." And the word was an indictment.

One night I received his telegram saying that he would be an hour late getting home. These came frequently, reproachfully, for he would not have been able to reach me earlier by telephone and thus, he would say, the expense of the wire (still delivered to the door). At DuMont I had met a girl I liked, an actress working as a secretary but trained at the Pasadena Playhouse; she was my age, irreverent, imparted to most things the double whammy of sex and humor, and she had told me that I could live with her if the going got rough. Reading Bill's telegram, looking down the years and seeing like statues all those images of us sitting out my life to Mozart, I began to pack. Such impulse is faster than the eye, faster than some varieties of time, for with packed bags and no forwarding address on the table, I caught up with the telegraph boy at the corner. "Bad news?" he asked, and I told him, "Crucial."

What had not been told me was that Bill Lesley and Ben Crowell, who had passed me along to the older man, had known each other in a place called Butler where both were recovering from near-fatal bouts with alcoholism. Finding me gone, Lesley went on a drunk and before he was finished he had consumed—but I will spare the reader this datum; I could not credit it then but can now, having lived to discover that capacity is increased by desperation.

The man had evidently found in me some idea of fulfillment—the end, or the beginning, of something that except in

fantasy was impossible. Even so he should have told me what
burden he was putting on himself with my unsatisfactory
presence for we were not lovers. A try had disclosed an
implacable incompatibility; since the age of consent I had
refused the role of Ganymede and if he could not be what
the sex ads call Greek Active he went without. Thus
underground pressures mounted upon more underground
pressures, the catamitic activity confined to the catacombs;
the nightly steam-letting, which is what sex is, was missing and thus the him-me-Mozart trinity assumed the most
earnest symbolism. Bill was not only Christian, he was
Germanic, so that wedded in his brain were the two most
authoritarian and elitist of doctrines: each act and word
carried for him a weight of Christian-Wagnerian implication; impossible to think of a man more pursued by myth,
legend, so thoroughly encircled by a ring. Though all his
references were not to the German myths; once when a lock
between rooms threw a tumbler and we were separated by
the relentless God-door, he talked softly to me through
the keyhole about Orpheus and Eurydice. I was the one with
the lyre but I could envisage me in the Orphic mists of his
mind with hair like gold silk, tunicked, androgynous at very
best. And I, sitting at his feet, in love with the music which
I always saw as gold-colored—spring sunshine or green-gold
river bottom light and always the odor of roses—I must have
felt the golden strands being woven around me, the increasing airlessness once the music was done. Our pot of soup,
never taken from the burner, from which we dined, throwing
in vegetables and meat and liquids from time to time; the
dark railroad flat; the celibacy; and the suppressed emotion,
for the word *love* was never used—all added up to a sketch
of a prison cell for us both and the bars were—were meant

to be—the golden music, most classical of devices to charm sailors and snakes and restless children.

Bill recovered and left New York to become curator of a famous museum in the Middle East. I have never seen him again. At the time of telling me about the near-tragedy brought on by me, a woman friend said, "I can never forgive you." I cannot share her attitude. If I had known about his weakness perhaps I could have been stronger; but only for awhile. Every move of mine in life that has seemed callous or cruel has been made solely because of a sense of suffocation, when the purple dust has gathered beyond a breathable density, when the air has just about been used up. Listening for the complaint of the door spring, not hearing it and its promise of liberating light and oxygen, I have taken the initiative, if that can be an adequate word for acts of sometimes panicked violence. I think each time I die, it is only *one* of the Twins, and thus I have had a kind of double life, my dual nature serving me as well thus far as a cat's nine lives.

Wallis Simpson was not the only duchess whose life touched mine. I met several Gräfins through Lesley, and to a mustached Frau they looked like my least favorite aunt, sister to my favorite. The favorite was handsome and propertied and clever; the least favorite was the spit and image of Tenniel's drawing in *Alice,* all jowl and scowl and cushion on the head and lack of education or delicacy. But her assurance was that of a duchess, which is what her severely browbeaten husband called her. A fragment of conversation and a short monologue will suffice to show how different in style the sisters were. At my favorite aunt's, in a pretty morning room set about with Louis Tiffany lamps and Boston ferns in long-legged wicker baskets and canaries in cages which were replicas of the house, an exchange between my aunt and another relative:

"And how is Aunt Flora?"

"Unfortunately she has quite lost her mind but otherwise is her old sweet self."

"Ah, as for that I don't imagine that one can too much tell the difference."

And from my least favorite, vast in her porch rocker, snuff leaking from her permanently disgruntled mouth (though, recalling her words today she very nearly becomes my favorite), a snippet of her endless monologue:

"I said Son better come on home now and see what's going on because his Mammy has been spendin money like a drunken sailor. Yestridy she said she was going to buy her some new pictures and blamed if she didn't go down to the ten-cent store and buy nearly every picture they had in the place."

It was on my favorite's very large farm that the mythical Shetland pony would have been stabled. I had no pony, but had my own horse there, named, by my aunt, Voltaire. There was a library through which I was invited to read my way— the most beautiful editions edged in gold, stamped in gold, bound in soft leather; here I became acquainted with Becky Sharp and Emma Bovary, with the Lintons and Earnshaws, the Ushers, with Gil Blas and Baron Charlus, with Grendel and Piers Plowman (and myself therein, Do Well); and with the Apocrypha and the thoughts of Origen and the tenets of Rosicrucianism and the *Kama-sutra*. Had she read these books? I do not know. She spoke of God, of speaking to God, of reprimanding God; and she spoke of her loathing for her husband. Years later I took as a token of sorts to her a girl with whom I occasionally slept. This girl asked, "Tell me, what are the arguments in favor of marriage?" And my aunt replied, "Property rights." She said about herself and her husband, "He married me for my social graces and I married him for his money." She professed to virginity. Again, I do not know. She bathed frequently in buttermilk and spread her skin with cucumbers, sliced as for a salad. She collected bone china and heavy Georgian silver, and box upon trunk upon wardrobe were filled with silks and moirés and taffetas by the bolt, some of them turning to dust when you touched them. The extensive attics of the house were a jumble of fine furniture and junk, with here a harpsichord and there a clavichord and yonder an elaborately carved parlor organ inset with pleated silk of a fragile rose color, bearing candlesticks on swivels; and naked or boxed there were guitars, lutes, a mountain harp, an Irish harp, a concert harp, and when one passed these twanged gently in the stirred air and from boxes came sympathetic vibrations of strings, and from heavy hooks in the ceiling there hung in muslin cages chandeliers which could sing like birds. Through the light, dustless air, for these attics were not dark but were set with dormers and skylights, one walked to music, which was altogether magical to a child. I dream of those rooms still, some of them paneled in fragrant cedarwood, others in a varnished-looking yellow wood that my aunt told me, with great satisfaction, came from the olive trees of Spain; the attics did not share one level floor but were on many planes and there were locked rooms into which I never looked, so that in my dreams they are like eternity. In one of my dreams. amid a forest of steamer trunks set on end I find a moldering leather bag full of guitar strings and masses of curly hair.

There were outbuildings almost as magical—one with a domed green roof from which, pointing at the heavens, protruded a broken telescope. My aunt had broken the instrument, saying only that she had not liked what she had seen, that it gave rise to a serious quarrel with God. In another outhouse there were troughs of straw into which you could plunge your hand and come up with a toy, but two things kept me from camping out there: the darkness of the place and the sorrow that emanated from my aunt when I pulled forth a marionette, a Pinocchio with the strings of its articulation snagged upon its nose.

I began going to my aunt when I was five years old. She was childless and my mother had six. My aunt would plead to borrow me (as she had borrowed others before me). In her large house filled with clocks competing with the ticking of deathwatch beetles in the walls I learned to be afraid of what can happen to your body in the dark (the twilit children's hour of home past for awhile), pains administered not by ghosts but by the terrible living. There was in that house, as too often there is, someone who had not had enough child-hood and wanted mine and took it, in increments of hours. Thus I was torn between wanting to escape my favorite house and wanting to escape my home. These two situations—the closet and the bed—were of and to my life the following: directives, muses, metaphors. Transcending them time after time has provided me with catharsis, continual (necessary) rediscovery of self-worth, and occasional art, which is the gleaning of squalor and the winnowing of fear: the real McCoy. If occasionally I fly (hello, Bill) it's because I've learned the labyrinth and earned my wings.

Recently I believe I bade Bill Lesley farewell. It was on a winter's day and I was watching my Jack Russell terrier play on her favorite slope behind the Metropolitan Museum and was assailed by the scent of roses, which invaded the contentment of my fugue state with astonishing force. I used amazement to retrace my thoughts and found that I had been comparing Daisy's play in the sunlight to the first movement (*allegro molto*) of Mozart's Fortieth Symphony. And there was Bill Lesley, his lean kindly face, his intricate personality. The January light on the slope, the innocence and splendor of my charming dog at play, memories of my youth, the museum—all conduced to summon the smell of roses and Lesley-Mozart-me. As I contemplated him he faded slowly, but his afterimage lingered as I walked home. Seeing through the bare trees the terrace of our apartment, I wondered if it would be the most courteous thing to ask him home with me, but in reply he winked out like the Cheshire cat.

It is just about here that two improbable persons enter my life. They are David Merrick and John Latouche. I am not inclined at this moment to extend charity to either of them, or even remote kindness; and so I will tarry awhile over Kitty, for whom I left Bill Lesley, and New York, and freedom: the first of my life's two true idylls.

Kitty was a small woman whose voluptuousness was something of a problem, being incomplete. Begin at her head: thick chestnut hair (at that time) which seemed to leap from her skull, properly above a wide forehead; big un-innocent eyes, one green, one blue, a slight cast giving her every expression a louche connotation; nice small nose happily not pointing toward a much too large mouth, the size, she said, giving men ideas she was glad to corroborate. She had a certain resemblance as a brunette to Dorothy McGuire, including what she called "the cleave in my chin." Moving on down this feisty personage (as most men were wont, and many women wanted, to do) we come to a strong columnar neck, that of a goddess; that photograph of Garbo with her head thrown back so far it is painful exposes the neck and throat of Kitty, whose shoulders too were Garbo-wide; skip now for good reason to the hips undulative from an eighteen-inch waist which after her cunt (Kitty's word) gave her greatest pleasure as became a Southern belle; her thighs were alabaster solid with the inner muscle, the sartorius muscle, strongly delineated, which she said was because her legs were so often and prolongedly stretched

49

open; the legs were just barely long enough but sufficed and were shapely and her feet were like most women's, gnarled. Her back was a great beauty—later in the nightclub act it was always completely bare to the tailbone of her callipygous arse; her elbows and knees were the focus of a ritual in which lemons were rubbed on, as her hair was treated with olive oil (by me, foreshadowing Vermont and a maharani and a twice-weekly ritual in the sun watched for all I know by coupling natives in the surrounding shade); Kitty also used honey for arcane purposes, and salt; oil, lemons, salt, honey—the result a woman of biblical allure, a Tamar, a Miriam. . . . Now what of Kitty have we in our verbal reconstruction elided? Ah, her as she would say tits. She did not have any, or scarcely any; the buttons upon her admirably broad chest were those of some adolescents, the tragic ones. She told of frantic kneadings, of consultations (in Savannah, her home) with Gullah-speaking black women and herbal "cures," one of which caused skin eruptions considerably larger than her nipples. . . . She even used, she said with painful solemnity, the vacuum cleaner to suck from her the submerged breasts and swore that the Hoover and not normal development was responsible for what she had had to settle for. Accustomed to flat brown chests I found little to wonder at in her boyishness but did agree that the heavy padding she used best complemented her lovely hips. The result of her natural abundance and the little bit of artifice was a real traffic stopper. To walk with her was to experience pride and humility, a daily experience for we walked from Perry Street to the DuMont Network in the mid-fifties and as she was "my girl" I was proud, and as she was "my girl" I was also insulted by the remarks of truck drivers and those men whose automobiles sidled near us at the curb so that they could name their preference as though she were a waitress dispensing trays at curbside. These men she called "chowhounds" for they always spoke of eating. I felt that I thus learned some of the burden of being a woman. I asked her if she was ever tempted to smash a face with anything at hand instead of smiling, smiling, and returning as she often did sexual remarks (at those times I felt most insulted, probably a sexist reaction in today's parlance). She asked me to reverse it and see how I felt—if it were women hooting and smacking their lips, or if the men directed their lust at me. I was able with real anger to say I would smash their goddam faces, for Louisville was not yet that far away. I remember her curious regard which said that she did not understand, and it was true that any advance, if she was in a position to return it, was returned. She was one of those women who truly needed men, even their sexual insults, and if one had spoken of objectification she would have hooted: who objectified whom? She was entirely in love with the male form and essence, with balls, cocks, tongues, the swagger that we have come to call "macho," the brutal *itness* of male focus that made a woman into an *it:* a cunt.

Our first Christmas together I went from the studio to the offices to pick her up, about five-thirty in the evening. I was late, she would not mind, both of us thinking of the gala evening ahead and the sweetly decorated room on Perry Street, of gifts, surprises. The dark was streaked with snow that was sticking alternating with sluices of sleet, the heavens with hush and whisper duplicating the sound of tires on Madison Avenue. I was late because I had with my new increase in salary (from $75 to $300 a week) bought Kitty a jewel, an unset ruby. Buying it I had imagined it in her navel, dangling from one ear, worn as a pendant, a diadem, but never in a ring. I had had her smiling a broad ruby smile, had

seen the ruby and a sister gracing her nipples, but never a
ring. The Village was filled with lovers and we were among
them, happily unmarried, living without strings or rubber
bands but with plenty of rubbers and Kitty had a diaphragm.
She did not like the feel of a sheathed cock but if the urgency
precluded that primary insertion she would watch impatient
and lascivious the unrolling of the condom. I had discovered
that to be without protection was dangerous for she did not
trust me to withdraw and with trip-hammer blows forced me
off her when she had miscalculated my timing, blows to the
face which left marks and bloodied my nose. Her franticness
was morbid, her distrust seemed pathological, and it was the
only unattractive thing I ever saw about her in a year of love.
As I never gave simply a simple gift, these thoughts were all
implicit in the ruby—the bloodied nose, her relief at the
onset of each menstruation. Once she asked bitterly, "What
would I feed a kid from, one of *these?*" and I had a glimpse of
how far-reaching that adolescent tragedy was.

In the office I found Kitty alone with all the workers gone
except for two black janitors, young men who swept and re-
swept around her feet, who knelt before her to polish desk
legs, burnish the wastebasket, and redo the whole job as un-
worthy. Kitty seemed amused and spoke endlessly in her
broadest Southern as though that too amused her. But when
we were ready to go and one of the young men asked in a
pleading voice if she would not kiss him Merry Christmas she
acquiesced with no hesitation and after a visible exchange of
tongues performed the same holiday pleasantries with the
second young man. I don't know if what I felt was perturba-
tion or thrill at this sight I had never seen before; certainly
there was electricity in my response, that neural coursing
of heated filaments that seems to be the result of watching

someone feel what you yourself have felt and thought it exclusive. I had discovered the tactile shock of black skins and tongues and muscles a few years before in the army; a man twice my age had, I guess the word is, seduced me in the middle of a moonlit Philippine field and since then I have been trying to understand what the crop of low-growing fragrant plants could have been, trying to find the knowledge tucked away in my mind along with the revelation of his satin-marble body and sweet mouth. We continued our affair for months, and when we were sent home together, we made love in a gun turret each night and formulated plans: I would get off the train with him in Indianapolis and live with him; to make this possible he would leave his wife and children. I was serious about him, that remarkable combination of lover and father, and believe that only the image of left children could have caused me, to his surprise and grief, to refuse to leave the train with him in Indianapolis. All the way from California, as we lay in our adjacent top bunks holding hands and kissing, afraid to do more—arrest at the last minute, scandal, dishonorable discharges (much low joking about that one)—I tried to fight off the faces of small black friends peering at me from the past, whose father my lover had become—this and not the uncomprehending sorrow of the kindly woman who was his wife changed the direction of my life. In the growing empathy I became one of the fatherless sons and nestled with my brothers four abed like fieldmice in their funky nest, as I had done in childhood when a storm kept me from making it home. I recalled how the presence in the next room of the black father was an absolute comfort, unlike the disturbing proximity of my father whose different darkness could seem more formidable than any storm, and concluded—because I needed to, because it was inevitable—that a black father is

53

more important than a white father because black children need more protection.

On impulse, seeing the men hiding their kiss-induced erections as they went to the restroom, I followed them and heard, as I opened the door, a remark about the "hot cracker bitch." I believe I had had it in mind to ask them home with us, or the one who had been so sincere, he of the pleading voice. The other young man had taken Kitty's largesse slyly. As I say, I believe it had been in my excited mind to hurry integration along in the gaily decorated room on Perry Street but in instances of lust recalled it is difficult to attach dates to certain refinements, and I had recalled and embellished that near-miss many times since. But Kitty and I, as we were destined to do, did finally make the breakthrough as two Southerners with a black man, and it is one of my best and most painful memories.

Kitty exuded the pungent odor of martinis, when naked and in the attitudes of love. She drank, but bourbon, and it was a mystery to me until I recalled the lemons which coupled with the briny odor of her excitement to produce a martini, which I lapped from her skin. Her perfume was astringent, citrusy, and may for all I know have had a gin base. As martinis were then my passion, to drink Kitty was a continuous pleasure. I don't know if she was insatiable; I never had the chance to find out; we leapt from beds of love to tear out into New York, devouring the Village, and, as my fortunes increased along with my modest fame (such a thing?—stories about me in *Down Beat, Look* magazine, *Coronet*—Elizabeth Taylor and I in the same *Look*—Tallulah Bankhead and I in some other magazine together—the company I kept!) Kitty and I ventured onward and upward to such as the Rainbow Room, to expensive seats on Broadway; we frequented Sardi's

as became two theatrical aspirants and probably because we
were decorative we were given better and better tables. We
were often asked upon leaving that place for our autographs
and would consult each other silently: What name to sign
tonight? She had signed Dorothy McGuire after a woman
assured her "I didn't know you were so pretty offscreen!" and
I signed, after a similar hint, John Agar; but we were both
chameleons and could get away with a whole spectrum—I
with Louis Jourdan and she with (after her hair change) Olga
San Juan, Betty Hutton, and once, incredibly for the hound
was French, with Michele Morgan. But Kitty experimented
upon herself with all the dedication of a girl expecting someday to do her own makeup ("No, *not* Perc Westmore; I am a
mistress of maquillage!") for the cameras. Hours before one
of our uptown hunting trips she would begin, big lighted
mirror on a trunk, she on the floor, a palette of colors any
painter might covet beside her. Came the night of the
Gleaming Bronze, a new color for hair which we understood
would wash out if you were not satisfied. Gloved, aproned,
masked (I think) against fumes, I performed the magic of
transforming my girl into a pretty good facsimile of Rita
Hayworth. What was left of the muck we smeared onto my
hair—mine only for an evening on the town. Glittering red-
bronze we drew more than the usual attention, some of it
decidedly not approving—those looks reserved for me.
Secure in heterosexuality, a defense whose importance can
never be overstressed, a revelation to a nominally homosexual man (as was being daily and nightly proved), I pressed
on against the hostility and had a good time and Kitty and I
took home a nice catch for her—I was not interested—and I
slept unperturbedly on my half of the bed while they, stacked
on her half, moaned in my dreams; for I was secure in knowing

that I would return to my own hair color and persona come morning. Alas. Was it Clairol I should sue, or my gullibility? Washing and re-washing only produced a more realistic bronze, bronze after weathering, a decided green. I was due at a Saturday rehearsal, unusual, but our star had only returned to town and we all needed to meet her and I needed especially to learn about her range and so forth before I wrote songs for her on the weekend, which we would rehearse starting Monday. We rehearsed four days and played live on the fifth, one and a half hours of terror on camera. Should I cap myself for the meeting? I owned no cap. Should I wear Kitty's shower hat? Seeing the entwined sleeping bodies sweaty and sticky in June and jism I had a flash of hatred for my lover whose gleaming bronze hair flowed upon her pickup's shoulder—flawless hair, the thatch of a goddess, my handiwork. But look what she had put upon my head (and nowhere in the thought did horns obtrude; we were free, we were unjealous, we were very fortunate in fact).

The cloudy June day extruded one ray of brilliant light which fell exclusively upon me as I walked into the rehearsal hall and faced Elaine Stritch where she sat tailor-style upon the grand piano. Those weekly companions of mine, for we were a television rep company, broke into applause at the green hair and the effect upon it of the sun. Stritch gave me her Tom Sawyer grin and added one more scalp to her belt.

She was in fact playing a frontier dance-hall girl who in the penultimate scene (before the clinch) had to shoot a lot of Indians. Long-legged as a colt in her micro-mini hoopskirt, she sang my song "Every Time Another Redskin Bites the Dust" while firing blanks at everybody including the cameraman. One line of the song should suffice: "As for Fleetfoot and Big Storm / How I wonder who'll keep their wigwarm"—

this was sung in a marvelous hillbilly whine. This show "introduced" Bea Arthur as a schoolteacher who takes off her
glasses, lets down her hair, and becomes beautiful, desirable,
and brave. Meeting her, we did not doubt that she was brave
for she was somewhat large; but the other two requirements?
She made it on camera with flags waving; that magic of
certain skins which take the lights and scrutiny of the camera
and transform them was hers, and those of us huddling at the
monitor all expressed astoundment in the same way, pause
followed by applause as though she could hear us away off
there on the stage. She and Stritch, who does often deserve
the misused "incomparable," made that one of our most
successful satires, for in the end it became believable, and
charming, and it was funny (my lyric example notwithstanding). We were beautifully reviewed and Stritch and I were a
new combination, platonic, I hasten to say, though not
because I failed to try. An impregnable fortress was our
Stritch and because I know her temper I will not go further
into revelations of a sexual nature, though I would like to.
That summer I went home to Kentucky for a little visit and
while I was there she was arrested in Central Park for taking
off her bra to sunbathe, and when I called her about it there
was already a change in her tone—national publicity will do
that to you; and though she performed many selfless acts for
me in the still-near future, such as recording a tape of a show
of mine for audition purposes, she did go on and disappear
eventually into that limbo that waits just the other side of
stardom's gate. The end for us came when I went backstage to
see her in a show that starred her and she said, unpleasantly,
"Oh, it's you" as though I were a tax collector. I mean the end
as far as I was concerned in the privacy of my vanished affection. I did go on and see her, and see her new apartment on

East Fifty-fourth Street with its hastily painted portrait of her, and its little bar foreshadowing her alcoholism, and I did listen to her say the sort of thing we had hooted at together on bicycle rides, lying in grass doing satires of Most Hated Types, drinking huge amounts of martinis in her apartment (her old apartment, shabby and comfortable). Attempting a satirical interpretation of her haughtiness, blasé affectations, and such remarks, made petulantly, as "I'm the happiest successful girl in New York," I intercepted, as one would intercept arrows, killing looks and saw that I had lost her as she had lost me. I have been through this so many times with people to whom fame arrives as an affliction that I see it, perhaps in their defense, as a concomitant of fame, as something unavoidable, as part of the bargain. The latest of my friends, a man already deservedly well-known, to whom this has happened following a great success in England and exposure to "the Faubourg" for a few months, was here, as a stranger, only a week ago. When I last saw him in 1983 he was an artist quite austere in his dedication as well as a fine critic. Last week (it is now May) I saw through great distance the petulance, heard the lies that allowed him to leave very early, felt the sorrow but faint now—not much blood left in the ancient wound. I have decided that for some people fame exposes an inner creature that was there all along making compromises, calculating one's worth in money or negotiable loyalty, making one a promise: Just you wait. When fame comes these ones turn inside out like gloves, the markers are called in, and the time of settlement is at hand. It is not that they have not always known "who" they were; it is that they did not dare risk showing it without the aegis of fame. Their discipline, dedication, hard work, grim self-denials: all so that they might someday be written about in *People* magazine.

Once there, see what happens: alcoholism, free-basing, Elaine's. And no work.

And in the meantime, Kitty and me, me and Kitty. She is at work while I cavort with Stritch, and intensely occupied when I am not there in the evenings, either exploring the reaches of her sexuality or plotting career moves with the help of whomever. As we often said, our room on Perry Street witnessed more auditions than the offices of Cheryl Crawford.

When I got home, if the door was doublelocked I went around the corner and had a drink or several, eventually making the telephone call that would be answered, and home I would go to compare notes. Immediately after sex Kitty was voluble and still excited; often I profited from this excitement and did not mind tasting the other man in her mouth. This courtesy of the right to doublelock and prolong privacy was mine too but I had no inclination to be unfaithful to her, beyond my essayal of Stritch; I certainly was not tempted to betray her—as I thought of it but did not think of it when it was reversed—with another man. It was just that I had had so much experimentation and she had not, and her wings, frightfully experienced-looking, were in fact fledgling.

A nice paradox was that she felt safe experimenting because I was there, and her lover. Thus men who might be tempted beyond the permissible had been informed beforehand that a lover was due home eventually and a picture of me, looking somewhat like Elvis Presley in the Bad Old Boy sullen demeanor of the satiric pose, was prominent in the room. Only once, some intuition led me to question the double-locked door and I rattled the knob and hit the frame, then waited in the stairwell to see what would happen. A very angry-looking man hurtled out and a scared Kitty crept down to find me and thank me. So scared was she that she was what it pleased us to call a good girl for over a week. But she never told me what it was the man had done or threatened, to reach out so powerfully and urgently prod my intuition on our behalf. All I was told was that he was from Hell's Kitchen and hung like a horse.

We had many such weeks in our year together, weeks that belonged exclusively to us. Some of the things we did: that year saw the revival of the thé dansant at New York's best hotels and we attended them all, fox-trotting, tangoing, rumbaing; being Southerners (as we said, safe in New York) we called everything that was not Latin or a lindy a round dance; round and around we went, singing in each other's ear, discreetly drunk, amorous, under the approving eyes of New Yorkers no more beautifully dressed than we, no more glamorous, not as young, with no more to hide. We took the Staten Island Ferry on hot late nights, back and forth, forth and back, quoting Miss Millay; we dipped into queer bars on Eighth Street, heard Mabel Mercer at the Bon Soir, Kaye Ballard at Le Ruban Bleu, were at La Commedia for Alberta Hunter's return to New York. Miss Hunter had been in Europe for perhaps twenty years and the grubby little Commedia was hardly an auspicious place for a comeback; before the name change it had been Tony's and was famous, but cramped and grubby withal, and an unfriendly air pervaded it. That night a comedian-impressionist named Sheila Barrett was head of the bill and we were there at her invitation. Once we were there she made it clear that we were not there as her guests, the sort of gratuitous remark in which she brazenly specialized, as in her act she had perfected bitchery and high camp. One of the musicians on my television show was there—a man who was also Ethel Waters's accompanist—and he, Reggie Beane, introduced us to Alberta Hunter. As is the case in many small clubs in New York, there is no proper dressing room and unless the artist is willing to sit on a john all the hours between sets she is generally to be found at a table with someone to keep her company. I performed this office for Lee Wiley when she was briefly at a handsome fly-by-night club called the Jickey, and for Mildred Bailey at the Bon Soir, though I think that place had adequate dressing rooms. Reggie was sitting with Miss Hunter but had to leave after the first show and asked if we would mind taking his place until we were ready to go. Both Kitty and I sensed something bad, something regrettable, in the atmosphere and when Miss Hunter did her first show there were loud interruptions from Sheila Barrett's table, laughter and remarks, so that they had repeatedly to be told to shut up—to only momentary effect. When Miss Hunter came back to the table she was sweating heavily and gave off an odor that Kitty and I agreed later on was the smell of fear. I had smelled it once before, just prior to a shooting in the bar in Louisville where I moonlighted as a pianist, researching the Haymarket for my musical; the smell came from the person who moments later was shot dead where he leaned over my green-painted piano, his eyes glassy as though the opaqueness of mortality preceded death by a moment; the bullet went through him and out and shattered the glass on the piano into which people put money, called the kitty. My Kitty had smelled the fear on her mother as they—father, mother, child—watched from their stopped car some terrible act by whites against a black man, in the deep night-breathing country around Savannah. We sat with Alberta Hunter through the night and after her last show we left with her. We wanted to see her home but she forbade it, saying, "Saint Nicholas Avenue at this hour of the morning? You children go on home and

remember"—a wink at me, a quote from one of her songs—
"one long steady roll!" A handsome woman, just in her forties
I imagine. She was around it seemed briefly, then gone and
not until her reappearance in the 1970s did one discover
what had happened to her.

Does one continue the montage of me-and-Kitty things?
They are many, and varied, but not infinite: jazz clubs, the
Beekman Tower for drinks, the Cloisters, the one-time-only-I-
swear-it trip around Manhattan with its melancholy-inducing
sights of ashheaps and squashed cars piled upon the shores of
its rivers; Manhattan is best seen from the ground, or a plane;
recovery from the boat trip is slow; one feels its clogged
arteries as one's own; the vigorous names—Spuyten Duyvil—
and legends, squared off against the reality of man's detritus,
which always wins. To have seen this island when all its
streams were rushing! streams now running beneath apartment houses and streets occasionally breaking through the
asphalt only to be subdued: this in a city perpetually in need
of water.

I always knew when Kitty had met someone challenging
and mentally would move aside leaving room, for it was in my
mind that I was most monopolistic of her and only there that
the words "I love you" were said. I had been an abused child
and an abused young adult (as we say nowadays) and being
reborn at twenty-four, I had vowed never to put another
human being before me or to allow one to seize precedence.
But with Kitty, to break my vow was easy, as in a Cole Porter
song; the kick she gave was champagne, cocaine, gin and
vermouth, for all of which one generally had to pay hand-
somely, but the perfect word is *gave,* and generosity, like
water priming a little meadow pump, brings forth the same.
To please her was my aim, I wore her colors to each daily joust

and was the stronger for it; in the smallish room on Perry Street—to move never occurred to us though we were very solvent—I never felt claustrophobic for in today's jargon she did not crowd my space; her sexual adventures with other men did not daunt me but may have enhanced our own highly satisfactory dalliance. The new man, the one who broke into the latest segment of our idyll, was a specialist: he specialized in menstruating women. Did he . . . I asked, tactfully allusive and she said, No, not that, but he loved to slip and slide around in it. She imagined it had something to do with being born (to him) she said, and of course he was perfectly safe. Kitty was quite vulgar in her speech but I am reluctant to quote her, for the mitigating charm and huge humor will be missing as will the radiance of the countenance—eyes raying health and gladness, little nose twitching like a rabbit's in glee over a fresh lettuce—which both supported and disarmed the filthy mouth. Recently a film of outtakes has been released and on it one of Carol Lombard talking dirty and in her I find restated the sweetness of Kitty at her Anglo-Saxon business, like a cross between the Abbess and the Wife of Bath. Let it go at that.

After what we called the Blood Bather (put on reserve for Those Special Days) we took a little summer jaunt to the Hamptons and cavorted there in what today would be considered remarkable privacy. The handsome beaches were sparsely populated, the few restaurants uncrowded, Montauk was a cluster of rough buildings with barely a motel among them and was my favorite of all the villages at the end of Long Island: all but forgotten since the flurry of the twenties, the great hotel empty, the skyscraper vacant; sandy, sunny, fish-smelling, briny Montauk, I wish I had bought all of you and kept you as you were, for you were my idea of Paradise, isolated from the languidly chic Hamptons as an eremite alone on his desert rock. When as a child I envisaged the ocean, it was the ocean at Montauk; and the fog there around the lighthouse: the fog and lighthouse as seen at Montauk become definitive. A small house with a blue door open- ing onto the wide beach and the sea; a diner; a store or two; a restaurant with two rickety tables teetering on the uneven sidewalk very like a snook cocked at East Hampton; and the scrubby growth and the gulls and the surf and the cool to cold night winds. Once having seen it we settled for Montauk. I remember beach plums. Increasing rockiness toward the Point. Declivitous cliffs eroded into nooky coves, an acre of lily pond lying surprisingly just atop a cliff within a few feet of the edge and the drop to the ocean. Bleeding feet. Real exhaustion. Exhilaration of the spirit, of the soul. Lying on the windy beach at Montauk I wrote a song which because I like it I will include in this account of the slowly closing book of our year (for it is now September and as we know, "the days dwindle down to a precious few— September, November . . . ." By November the bliss is gone forever).

(Begin with ad-lib patter about the frog who when asked what he will do after graduation says he will go to East Hampton and be social, and he is hooted down by his classmates who tell him warts are not acceptable in East- and Southampton. He is very disillusioned. And then one day:)

> The frog from Quogue
> Met a lawyer
> Who told him leopards
> Had changed their spots
> By filing

A Star-Bright Lie

All the proper papers
In all the proper
Courts.

He guaranteed
That froggie would be
An enormous success
In South- or Easthampton
As soon as he lost
His warts.

   So froggie paid his fee
   And true to the guarantee
   He was declared
   As free from warts
   As a frog could ever be

The frog from Quogue
Threw a party
And told his friends
That with the morning
He'd leave for foreign
Ports
He was the gladdest frog
That ever went out of Quogue.

The frog from Quogue
Went down to East Hamp-
ton and joined some clubs
And established credit
In all the stores
So when he went out
He would always be properly
Dressed.

Coleman Dowell

His charm, his wit
His erudition
Were much admired
And so he was popular
As you've probably
Guessed.

    Then one day at the club
    When he
    Was sipping a B & B
    Somebody said
    That's a dirty frog
    Now it's either him or me

When he got home
The Chamber of Commerce were
Waiting there
And they told him that
They were sure he understood:
He was the maddest frog
That ever went out of Quogue.

    The frog from Quogue
    Went back to the town
    Of his birth and opened
    A shop for gentlemen's wear
    And tried to drum up trade
    With all of his old
    Cohorts.

    But other frogs
    Refused to buy
    What he had to sell
    Because it was rumored
    About that he had
    No warts.

A Star-Bright Lie

So now he's digging ditches
In a pair of dirty britches
On the outskirts of East Moriches:
He's the saddest frog
That ever went out of Quogue.

Riding horses from the oldest ranch in America we essayed the Sound side. We left at 4:00 A.M. for deep-sea fishing. Then all at once we both wanted Manhattan and returned on the Long Island Railway. In a changing world . . . good to know that some terrible things never change. Etc.

But we, not being terrible, had changed. Our longish intimacy at Montauk had I think frightened us. Kitty missed a period, nothing to worry about (but we both remembered a certain night of many wonders).

One early morning at the Christopher Street stop I tumbled out the subway door drunk and half asleep. The motorman leaned from his caboose. "Black and beautiful" was not yet in the language but he was both. I went with him under the river to Brooklyn on my knees in the caboose, then the notion, the conviction, took me that this paragon just might unstop Kitty's plumbing with such a plunger, the way you would unstop a sink. I told him I did not want to drain him and told him why. I described Kitty. Yes, he was the proper gent for her. We rode home from Brooklyn, or wherever it was we left the train, in a taxi. I asked Kitty to see what I had managed to bring her, never mind the smallness of the hour. My crudeness did not affect them. A civilized drink was had by all, a bit of chatter. I fell carefully onto my side of the bed and fell asleep. Their love, being a first for both of them—his first white woman, her first black man—went on for a long time, eventually and authoritatively invading my sleep, so that I

67

had the choice of voyeurism, no favorite of mine, or participation. I chose the latter.

By November we know that Kitty is pregnant. The question is, black or white? The question is—only for her—to abort or not to abort; I say over my mutilated body. Then as now, only the most extreme circumstances would lead me to acquiesce in what I can't help seeing as murder. Genius lights randomly; suppose it was meant to be a Beethoven, an Einstein (and on and on). I believe that everyone I know favors hacking the kid out nowadays, so much so that it seems to have become the point of pregnancy: abortion rather than birth, a new biological wrinkle, the way womanhood (and manhood) is proved. But it was still a serious matter in 1951.

Kitty and I became domestic. Our room had no kitchen, only a half-size refrigerator by the bathroom door; I bought an oven to fit over a two-burner stove and began to learn to cook. I don't know why. She was healthy and capable of running from one end of Manhattan to the other. But I imagine that it was our way of saying good-bye to each other, of giving the kid a little taste of Mom and Dad at home before it was born. For we knew what we were going to do. Kitty's long-sought chance came coincident with the pregnancy—a revue in England planned conveniently for the following fall. If the baby was on time she would have recovered by the onset of rehearsals and according to our plan Kitty would be in England ready to go. Her parents were very young, her mother only sixteen years older than Kitty, her father only seventeen. They would be the parents. The birth would be in England. Up until the departure from Savannah Kitty's mother would mime pregnancy, the nursery there would be refurbished, everything—Savannah, friends' minds, the very air—would be padded like a bassinet. How beautiful! Kitty's mother exclaimed; I always dreaded being a grandmother!

Cable from England: WHITE. SPIT AND IMAGE OF FATHER. LOVE.

We named him Christopher Townsend. Except of course we did not, any more than the name I have given to her, Kitty, is her real name. Here the purpose is really to protect the innocent for we all agreed he must remain so and never suspect that the man he met when he was twelve was his father. Kitty went on to become a movie star—his sister the movie star, you understand, and I doubt if he has ever given a thought to the possibility of duplicity. I imagine if she writes her memoirs she will be as selective as I have been and I doubt that even in senility her parents will suddenly decide to reveal to him the truth about his real parents—whatever that means; something other than furnishing sperm and egg, I imagine. And so we are all safe. If that's the object. I know we thought so at the time.

After England, pre-Hollywood, Kitty turned to women as her love objects. I had been frightened in Louisville by a pride of lesbians and had never recovered, so the news was unpleasant to me. In Louisville the girls had all resembled Fran Lebowitz; they swaggered squatly, fought with ice picks, and stuffed rolls of socks in the front of their pants. They linked arms around pianos and bawled songs about ass-holes. Some of them drove trucks. A highly admired, in New York and elsewhere, Louisville belle was said to be of their number. But I was not reassured by her femininity and imagined Kitty with one of the Lebowitz look-alikes, think-ing with foul heterosexual despair that the mother of my child was doing that.

When I at last saw Kitty and my successor—across the street, Kitty now wearing her great blonde bell of hair that was to be her trademark—it was evident that they were very much, as Kitty used to say, "in like" with each other and the older woman's femaleness afforded me shameful relief, for surely it's the love that matters? But try to tell that to the Charles Socarides of the world—and I was one, just then.

Still, gossip has it that it was Kitty's honest but blatant lesbianism that brought to an end her movie career. She was a real actress, a surprise I have never quite got over, and I hear that she is playing the Russian parts on stages from the Coast to Louisville. I would have liked very much to have seen her Arkadina.

To leave Kitty as an aging Russian won't do. I'll mention a few of the times when she delighted me, not too hopeful that the charm will survive bare transcription. One time I was relating to her how I had bested someone so thoroughly that he "just threw up his hands." I saw a look of horror on her face. "Threw up?" she said. "You mean he had *eaten* his own . . . ?" Another time we're in a drugstore for a sandwich. We give our orders. The waitress howls out Kitty's request: "BLT on white, hold the mayo." The sandwich comes and Kitty checks it carefully: "Plenty of B, lots of T, no mayo. Shit, they forgot the goddamned L." And Kitty on the telephone: "I'm just wearing perfume. Why not come and take me in fragrante delicto?"

Naked, fragrant. I'll leave her there.

I have never abided by a clear logic and so I had my
nervous breakdown before and not after I met David
Merrick. How I met him is not the point; the point is, a
David Merrick lies in wait for all people like me, to try to round
off in our adult lives what murderous brothers and incestuous
uncles were not able to complete in our childhoods because
we somehow learned to grow fast and outgrew them. I have
sometimes wondered if Merrick was in fact a result of my
breakdown, one of its abiding phantoms, peculiar to me and
the aftermath of my illness; but too many people have seen
him for that to be quite so, though many of those claim that
they too believe him to be a hallucination. But before I say
anything unkind about Mr. Merrick let me state emphatically
that I think he made a real contribution to the Amurrican
Theater. Consider *Happy Hunting* for a moment. And the rise
in seat prices. *Maria Golovin!* That tremendous write-off kept
him solvent, one heard. The theater was to David Merrick
what dog manure is to Mare Edward Koch: a chance for self-
aggrandizement. His productions, with a few exceptions,
were like Koch's Trump Towers: high places from which to
get a better look at themselves in the waters below. I knew

Merrick; I knew him very well; there was a time when instructions were given to his wife that I was the only person to be admitted into their hotel suite. I was to be his Rodgers and Hammerstein rolled into bite-size hors d'oeuvres and sprinkled with a mince of Cole Porter. He managed to give me fifty dollars a week for a while, this to be taken from my "advance," through collusion with the really corrupt Local 802: he told them I was a cello player, I told them I could not even hold the instrument properly, they gave me membership as a cellist, and I was put on a payroll, member of a mythic orchestra in a theater housing a non-musical comedy. This thing of theaters maintaining so-called orchestras on their payrolls even though a drama is playing the house is a union, and not a Merrick, idea; but it could have been a Merrick idea, it bore his unmistakable stamp. But before I enter the intricacies, like the figure in the carpet, of the Merrick mind, I must return to my own mind and its excursion below the border ("everyone goes South every now and then" —Billy Joel).

I was still writing for television and had been on it myself, a brief appearance on Roberta Quinlan's NBC show. Miss Quinlan was then the highest-paid TV performer, a pretty girl with a small lilting voice and the easy manner of someone performing at home. She introduced a song of mine, a publicity gimmick to get us both in *Look* magazine. Following my few minutes on camera I was tailed on the street for weeks by two adolescent girls, one of whom was certifiably crazy; it was her aim to kill me; she told me so whenever she got near enough to speak softly. The other one soothed her friend and assured me that the girl was just kidding. The crazy one, spying me far down a street, would let out a yell— "There's that television actor!"—and stick out a great fat tongue, and from whatever distance I would hear the vibrations of her Bronx cheer. Once when I came out of a house where I had dined I saw them lurking back in the shadows of Carl Schurz Park and the cry the mad one (assuming the other was just a tiny bit sane) gave was the whimper of a hunting dog when it first catches the scent of the quarry.

Certainly the awareness of those two lurking around contributed to my total insomnia which had begun with the birth of the child. I would lie awake feeling endangered because I believed he was. I thought he would instinctively know that his father was not the one who held him, nor his mother the one who obviously could not suckle him. My conviction grew in the night like something poisonous that as soon as the switch had been made in London, from Kitty to her mother, he had known the despair of desertion and that it would disfigure him, split his personality. And it came about that when I thought of him I could not think without effort of a singular being, for it was as if I had been the father of twins, one of them invisible, the doppelgänger of his brother. This shadow-baby had remained with Kitty, in her arms, and all his life long our son would look back and envy his shadow. And I would see the shadow-child growing up between Kitty and the one who was supposed to have been me but was a travesty and both the shadow-boy-man and the visible son would sense me as one senses a ghost, or a limb that has been removed.

I lived as a shadow with someone for awhile, himself so vague that I can only recall his last name, which was Mayer. His apartment was in the Village somewhere but finding it each time was a mild surprise. It was a place to which I went because I was needed there, needed to lie upon the bed before the fire and be worshiped. The walls of the room were a shade of black-purple called charcoal purple and the firelight threw shadows upon them and the ceiling which I contemplated through the hours of ritual, which however long could never satiate the young man. He fed upon me, but sweetly, as I had fed upon Kitty; and yet he could not move me. His need could draw me back to him nearly every night but I was unmoved by his yearning. He was driven into panic by my remoteness, so afraid of losing me that I left him. When I went to leave the key in the apartment I found upon the hearth many pages of philosophical ravings, some of which I believed I understood; but that I was their dark heart left me unmoved.

As part of my progression South I will include here the beginnings of a story I tried to make of the events and moods of that time. (And if South means madness it must also stand for the direction I was taking from music toward fiction, for my daily notations were no longer of songs alone but of themes which could only be developed in prose. I have them still, boxes and boxes of themes and ideas and, often, spurious journal entries of a person unknown to me but—how shall I put it—beginning to be suspected; that is, the journal entries of the writer I was to become, all the events of whose life would need to be invented, or evolved.)

Here is the fragment, thirty-two years old as I write this on June 27, 1984.

It was really amazing to me the way they all shut up when I walked into the room, as though they had been talking about me. Which was impossible, for I knew no one there. I had told Lal that I would meet her there at such and such an hour, a necessary vagueness because I had forgot to write down the time and, as usual, I had forgot the name of the hour. In this time and place— winter, city—the hours look so much alike that it is impossible to recall their names. I could actually only

Coleman Dowell in the early 1950s

Top: Kenward Elmslie, Dowell, John Latouche, and a friend's daughter. *Bottom:* Latouche, Dowell (standing), and Harry Martin, summer 1955.

Dowell photographed by Carl Van Vechten, 27 January 1957

Dowell photographed by Van Vechten, 26 February 1957

Van Vechten and Dowell, photographed by Van Vechten's assistant, Saul Mauriber, 26 February 1957

Doris Julian, photographed by Van Vechten, 4 March 1958

Kim Hunter, photographed by Van Vechten, 11 October 1960

Dowell and Daisy, photographed by Christopher Cox in 1984

name four to begin with: dawn, noon, dusk, midnight.
These are the stars, so to speak, and one makes obeisance
to their fame. Still, at times in the past I have been
confused about two of them when we met, for dawn and
midnight often dress alike and wear the same air of weariness,
a fashionable pose. In the light of winter even noon and
dusk can be mistaken for each other.

I walked into the room or rather onto the balcony
which overlooks the room and cast my gaze about for Lal.
It was then the assemblage fell into a musing kind of
silence, all with faces lifted upward to where I stood. It
was highly embarrassing for me, those, as it turned out,
several moments, and the only way I could bring them to
an end was to break a glass gently against the railing. The
pieces fell softly to the carpeting below and I was left
holding the stem from which intimations of its former
shape grew like memory.

They all turned away then and began to talk, chattering
animatedly as though they had got what they were waiting
for. Regret is foolish, but I do not shy away from it
because of that, and I was regretful that I did not (had
not thought to) seize the opportunity to confide in them.
Suppose I had said to them, when I held them in thrall,
said simply and without accusation or self-pity, merely
confiding to faces that might take on other aspects—of
friendliness or at least of interest—suppose I had said,
"When I went to put on my shoes this morning someone
had put small snakes in them, one in each." Having
caught at their imaginations I could then have gone on to
the other more difficult phenomena, more difficult because
small snakes are readily available in the shops, and my
apartment, I have come to believe, is even more accessible,
for shops have hours at which they close and my apartment, apparently, has not. That *I* have difficulty finding it
is no indication that others have the same trouble. From
the debris and artifacts left behind them, it is in fact clear
that they find my place easier to get to and use than their
own. Someone, not I, certainly, is overly fond of absinthe
and my well-known even temper has been severely tried
by evidence of such gluttony. Sometimes pills are left

75

scattered on the hearth rug along with dangerous-looking pieces of charred wood and I have found booklets of fine paper on my coffee table, and once, in an ashtray, a little pipe of good workmanship, Far Eastern, I would have thought.

But these, for all the carelessness of the charred wood on the rug, are appurtenances of civility and I do not quarrel with them beyond questioning their right to have been placed there in my absence. The bloodfilled stocking in my bathroom sink is another matter, as is the noose above my bed, so precisely hung that when I put myself on the bed beneath it and then sit up abruptly, it fits about my face and beneath my chin like an old-fashioned bonnet with tie-strings.

These are the least of the phenomena which have accumulated in my apartment as though I shared it (such is the evidence of another's fetish-filled life) with some-one(s) of Collyer Brothers persuasion. The newspapers with circled headlines pertaining to murders—stacks of these. The esoteric knife with gutting hook, the rare-looking firearms, the cache in my hall closet of grenades. And the bottles with alcohol-buoyant chancres. These last assault my vision with never-diminishing loathesomeness when I open my medicine cabinet. Once I could bring myself to examine them I saw that they had been removed from whatever source with the greatest skill, the tissue so neatly severed and trimmed that a great surgeon might have had cause to be envious.

One bottle contains an eye, blue, that revolves from the vibrations of the opening cabinet door, which has to be jerked apart from the facing to which it clings like a lover. The eye circles its bottle as though its business, like Emily Dickinson's, were circumference. In a moment of levity it occurred to me that it was there to keep watch on the chancres, which might otherwise . . . but I do not know what chancres not under strict surveillance do. That blue eye can see in the dark, I am sure of this, and thus it may be a noble experiment, or part of an experiment whose goals are lofty. The evolving, even in a bottle, of an eye that could see in the dark must be ranked with the search for fuel, in a place where darkness and cold are on the increase at a gallop.

Much later, with health restored, I saw the foregoing as an unconscious parody of a Poe fragment and tried, thrifty Scot that I am, to salvage it, and though the attempt was finally abandoned, I will include it here for it contains the seeds of self-commentary which would grow into what some have called my "style," and certainly contains my first try at polemics.

Continuing the above:

I dislike these bizarreries for another reason quite apart from their intrinsic nastiness. The blood in the stocking, the chancres, noose, floating eye, evidence of drug use and alcoholism, snakes, hints of amnesia, and terminal hostility and small acts of violence, are among the trappings of a kind of literature I disliked even in its heyday, which coincided with my youth and was the despair of it: the Southern Gothic novel.

I was born Southern but with a mind capable of coolness and logic, which, it seemed at the time, was not shared by any of the young writers who were then making their mark. "Storytellers," they were called, sometimes in defense, more frequently in offense, and I had to agree because when I was a child a storyteller was a liar. Over the years I met several of these storytellers who had gone on to great reputations and discovered that they were liars in life as well as in "literature," which severely affected for me their worth as artists. The projections of a reasonably balanced mind into that of, say, a murderous madman, when convincingly pulled off, is a feat worthy of attention, whereas the recital of his deeds by a real madman who has committed murder belongs in court, psychiatrists' offices, Krafft-Ebing, and may even make what's called compulsive reading, but is not, I think, literature. Equally, a person who lies out of compulsive need and has managed to learn to type does not add up to art, literature, or even skill except where the typing is concerned.

I am a border-state Southerner with connections on the
Delta, and I am aware of the considerable differences in
the quality of life in the two places, mainly as pertains to
respect for laws in what might be called high places, a
touchy subject since the decline and fall of Washington,
but I am now referring to the good ol' days, or to the time
of illusion that there were any such. It was during that
time that the Southern Gothic novel caught hold of the
nation's willingly neurotic attention and this spawned
such excess that a Nero/Caligula/de Sade would have
fainted with envy at the recountals of daily life below the
Mason-Dixon line.

Every state has moldering old houses, measureless
swamps, dwarfs, idiots, and drag queens, but below the M.-D.
line this apparently is status quo for the average cross-
roads village. There amnesiacs wander swinging bloodfilled
stockings, drinking into one corner of the mouth and
smoking dope out of the other, with a chancre in a jar
and a murder-headlined newspaper wrapped around a piece
of bacon and cold cornbread, heading on home to lie
beneath that symbolical noose and wonder what time it is.
They're nearly always missing something—an eye, for
example—and somebody else down the road has got it, if not
in a jar, then impaled and sticking up from a pincushion,
or in a pretty little box. Snakes slither about and get put
in Aunt Shug's shoes, which accounts for the frequent screams
heard in Southern houses. This all may, indeed, be Deep
South behavior. The snakes are surely real. And when
Deep Southeners come up Nawth they go crazy at the big
Yankee party and break something, shriek out something
unintelligible that the folks back home would be able to
interpret, or dive out a window tormented to death by
memory and incestuous longing in the shape of a bird.
Sometimes, if the neighborhood doesn't run to large terminal
parties, the Southerners get their necks twisted in tene-
ment staircases by uppity Nigras. In a more peaceful time,
in the compassionate imagination of a Southern sympathizer,
one of them actually got away and went back home and
ate peaches, high up in a leafy window with sexy, innocent
boys below calling to her in soft voices.

However, it's pointless to postpone with young scribblings the onset of my very real sickness, and so here goes.

I lived with a pack of actors for awhile, in Alexander Woolcott's old house beyond Ninth Avenue. The ground floor was a rehabilitation center for the insane. There were several floors, many rooms, a handsome drawing room in which Mrs. Pat Campbell had stolen food for her dog, in her delapidation not wondering why she found upon the tea tray such things as would please a dog, for Woolcott could be discreet. This and other tales were recounted as only actors can when talking of themselves. I left them with no backward glance (and no memory of a single face or name) and moved to Gramercy Park to my own studio apartment. All of this and the writing of the show, and what living I managed in the cracks between, is remembered in the flickering light of a nearly destroyed print of a movie. As I recall now those weeks and months, they too are vaguely defined so that I can't reconstruct how much time was actually spent in this pursuit—of a route or doorway into the actual hot country below the border for it was a trip I had to make before I could turn back around and I believe that I knew this, and knew I would recover. But that conviction belongs to now; then I was simply lost. People asked what I was "on." A rumor went around that I had become a drug addict. The first thing the person I have lived with for thirty years heard about me was that I was an addict; the second was that I was a sadist. I believe that I turned cruel, but there are no survivors for me to question. I have what may be a *fausse mémoire* of blood on the marble stairs at Gramercy Park.

I began to sob dry sobs that would come over me like hiccups without warning. Unfortunately they were not silent and dry, unsilent sobs in the Oak Room, on a Fifth Avenue bus, at a rehearsal, during fellatio, can profoundly disturb the one you're with. A child's whistle used on the show—the episode was built around a brat-turned-angel—was the catalyst, road sign, propellant—all of which will do to describe what occurred. The whistle lodged in my brain and went home with me tootling gaily, then in the night less so, then sadly, then horridly. Sometime or other I made a transition and when I came to, I was in Louisville staying in the carriage house of an acquaintance. One day we went to the country— it was autumn—and across a field I saw fox grapes weighing down a tree and started across the field to pick them, an old passion, and was plunged back to childhood and a similar day when I had stood on a split rail fence picking and eating grapes and looked at the swampy field I had just crossed and saw hundreds of black undulant objects and believed they were the limbs of murdered Negroes reaching for justice, before I saw that they were black snakes. In that field near Louisville I relived before the horrified eyes of my acquain- tance that day and what had informed it: the night of the bloodhounds, of the ax and the thick blood and clumps of hair in the cabin. She had been combing her hair. A white woman. There was blood in the comb for like a beheaded chicken running around she had gone on combing her hair for a minute afterwards, that is what they said. She had cut out of her belly the Negro's baby and he had cut off her head and that night he was lynched. Inhabiting both fields at once, and the London (no doubt) of Jack the Ripper and my child, I screamed myself voiceless. There's nothing, they tell me, more cathartic than a good scream. I began to recover though I was for a time afflicted by something like aphasia, except my version was more logical. Reaching for *plateau* I would come up with *tableau;* reaching for *place* I would settle for *play.*

A Star-Bright Lie

At the airport I asked for a one-way ticket to Grievance, Ohio. This was Cleveland, where I remembered it snowed all the time. Before I left, my friend trusted me with his car for a couple of days and I drove to my deserted wilderness home. To the rutted clay roads alongside sere cornfields, to the vine-hung swamps and springs rising from rock and hill and rushing through cellars of houses in our water-blessed world; to the stands of hickory nut, called scaly bark in my youth, and black walnut trees, and sassafras and mayapples whose roots I dug and sold by the pound; and to memories of great tracts of goldenrod bordered by the scarlet of sumac and the waves of perfume of honey locusts and to the ghost of the felled honey tree into whose golden cavern I crawled tearing out and passing along great chunks of molten sage and locust and clover; when I emerged, molten myself, I gathered to me a black, hooded cloak of bees, the cloak, someone said, shivering as though in a high wind; but of how I came to be divested of my deadly garment I have no recollection. Like a wary animal I circled a vast house whose hundreds of massive shutters were rudely nailed tight, crisscrossed with broken pieces of wood flaking green and blue paint and two-by-fours and split rails so that the house looked like the ghostly sutured remains of an operation by some butcher surgeon. As always was, as always will be, the air there was pervaded by the ineffable smell that gave the house its name, Sweet Brier. The odor was scarcely diminished even by the deep freeze of winter for it imbued the wood of the house and the brick and stone of it, its tall, squat, ornamental and plain chimneys, its woodlands, its outbuildings, waterways, the walls of its gardens, its walkways, hedges, the fenceposts of its pastures. There is a stretch in Central Park which in late spring—but no, I am here, not there now; here where my heart is like some deep-bedded fieldstone too heavy, too rooted to be moved, and it is in the surrounding fields that I sleep in my down-filled bag, like Wayland's feather boat, where I conjure the rustle in corn shocks no longer guardians, cairn-like, of the suspended house; and hear in the stealth of autumn winds low in the grass my own footsteps on Halloween night, and in the cries of birds I hear again our soft warnings to each other as we go about the business of our mischief. Each night I move my bed and blessed by the white moon—harvest? hunter's?—I survey the stony cliffs of the house's facades and precisely like a cartographer working from memory I map the stilled world within the walls, tracing with carefully detached memory the long tributaries of corridors, the estuaries of halls and landings, coves of rooms, noting always the emotional equator, shying from it, noting only its parallels and degrees of latitude. One would be safest in that closetless tower as high as that distant bluff; moving in the house's geography south, it is possible to feel the laxation of security. It seems that to pass from one part of the house into another via the enclosed breezeway connecting the ancient dwelling of logs encased in cosmetic rose brick with the later, more pretentious additions of pale stone, is like the passage through the Miraflores. To my ears the immensity within was clamorous, resounding at times like a cistern to whispers and cries metaphysically retained, and the sounds of games, serious, light, disgusting; innocent and criminal; a plumbline dropped through the emotional depths of the house would come to rest on neither bottom nor ledge. I saw on my last night of contemplation that it was unfathomable. I climbed at dawn to the top of the distant bluff where within a circle of alders my kin lay, their places staked out by mossy stones, some dating back to before the Revolutionary War. From that vantage point the slave-built walls marking the county's boundary could be seen, and beyond it halfway across the next county, to my aunt's farm lying among its buildings like some abandoned watering place in the maze of ponds, lakes, streams, glinting one felt unblithely. The cabins all about the countryside, deserted since World War II, basked and trembled in the late autumn sun and wind like half-animate objects of dull silver and tortoiseshell. Finally I went to the spired chapel on what we children had called the Green Grass, on whose steps I once sat in cold sweat trying to fathom eternity, burning forever: on and on (I said then) and on, while discomprehension grew. The words through repetition became entirely meaningless like their context and I have settled more or less for that; call it my religion.

Soon one of the two etesian winds would rise (the other, nattering like a succubus at the base of the skull, blew in March), and rise steadily toward its solstitial roar, no halcyon days for my wilderness home, bringing with it from mountaintops the bridles and blinders, the whips and reins of sleet to harness and command the snow horses, their great manes tossing and streaming upon the wind as they breached mountain passes. Even now the neglected orchards heralded their progression by hurling like petrified roses upon its path the last and sweetest of their apples upon which I, empty for two days, gorged, a carpophagous ghost haunting my own life. I wished to be the cambium between the hard shell of the world and the enduring fiber of that wilderness so that both might because of me regenerate: the fiber juicier, the shell more flexible and useful.

I dispute whoever first said you can't go home again. You can't *not* go home again unless you have a prefrontal lobotomy. It's just that once there you may as I have set formal language between you and it, "it" being the re-experiencing which is often sentimental. In the mapping of the house, for example, I avoided mention of the kitchen for one thing would have made and now makes the remembrance sentimental: mention of the four cakes which were always mellowing there, replaced as soon as eaten. Those cakes were wonderful: a jam cake, a chocolate cake, a coconut cake, and an angel food variously iced, this one "for the ladies." And behind the kitchen the smokehouse. Bacon. Ham. Aged sausage in casings a meter long. And further back henhouses, turkey pens, the duck pond, and behind them, fed by droppings, gardens, fields, patches and beds, cornucopias of richness; and root cellars, and dairies, and brooks running with trout and so on back to the big river and its catfish and up the slopes beyond to nut and persimmon and pawpaw trees and the endless largess of the wilderness, its wild berries and rosehips, fox grapes, medicinal roots, herbs from which oils were drawn and powders pounded; and from the foothill of the mountain one looked down upon the cultivation, the orchards in rows, the stables in settlements, the barns in communities; the soap house with its cauldrons hanging from tripods in the yards, the long low wash house like part of a musical instrument from which the clotheslines radiated like strings for the wind to play upon; the isolated privies; the flower gardens; the summer kitchen with its high covered walkway to the dining room, its rafters hung with glass wind chimes. In that stone-floored neat building over there are churns for making butter—undreamed of in Manhattan—the churn house, separate from the dairy which was separated from the creamery where butterfat was tested in tubes and on scales, a 1920s refinement that afforded a paying job to some family member, always female. And set apart, downwind, the pigpens abounding in mud, edged by the slopping troughs. Working again toward the house one encounters geese, guineas, and raucous peafowl, and the sheepfold with its long-unused gallery-like house in which wool was once carded, and somewhere in that collection of utilities is the flax house, and somewhere over there the grape press, the sorghum press . . . and so we are back to food again: the baby recalls the plate on which sorghum and butter are swirled together (later in boyhood he finds the same configuration and colors in a prized taw, amber and gold) and the warm soft biscuit sopped in the creamy lake and pressed to its mouth by a dark brown hand, this weaning food accompanied by crooning sounds, a wordless song.

One night in Cleveland my relative asked me if I was not curious about my old television show. It was the first I had thought of it and the question returned me with a jolt to the world I had left. It was also well-timed—for it was the night of the show.

On the screen unfolded the legend THE ALBUM OF UN-FAMILIAR MUSIC and the photograph of me doctored to look like a portrait adorned the cover of a large book. Its pages began to turn. The show was a recap of my career, an "and then he wrote" show with the highlights from each musical satire and the best song of that particular evening. Many of the original performers had been recruited including two Metropolitan Opera stars who had played and now replayed the Beast and his sexy blonde mother in our send-up of Cocteau's *La Belle et la bête.*

And here was Charlotte Rae re-recreating her mermaid in another spoof, singing "Like a Fish Out of Water"; and here was the brat-turned-angel sporting on Olympus singing "Ye

Gods and Little Fishes"; and Tyree Glenn, the great jazzman, as a crazed surgeon on Mars rubbing his hands, antenna bobbing, saying to his exotic scrub nurse, "Gimme sumpin *sharp,*" and the love song from that show, "Galaxy of Love"; and Sondra Lee, later Tiger Lily in *Peter Pan* on Broadway, stomping out the hoedown I had written for her Mammy Yokum role; and good-looking red-haired Bernice Parks of the nightclubs very effectively moaning my beguine "So Little Time." At the end of the hour and a half the cast lined up for the camera and all got down on one knee and said in unison, "Wherever you are, Cole, please come home."

My relative understood that I must leave. She and her family helped me very much. I was able to play unmorbidly with the children and when awkward moments came they had all been discreet about it. Or so I thought. But recently I talked to one of that family about the days I had spent with them and she, now a woman nearing forty, told me none of them had suspected anything. Still, I cling to my analysis: they were all discreet about it, and still are.

I was taken to David Merrick by his first wife, Leonore. A fat publicist of the day, Alfred Katz (among his clients, the Duchess of Windsor), said of the transaction: "David was going to divorce Leonore but she found Cole for him."

As none of this is probably recorded anywhere except on this paper, you are asked to take my word for it that the properties Mr. Merrick intended for me were *The Matchmaker* (*Hello, Dolly*), *Destry Rides Again* (*Destry*), and Gypsy Rose Lee's autobiography, which became *Gypsy.* Jerry Herman got the first, Harold Rome the second, and Stein and Sondheim the third. But our first project, for which Merrick had taken as co-producer Jo Mielziner, the set designer, was to be *Ah, Wilderness!* by Eugene O'Neill. I have to say that I do not admire O'Neill except for the film and TV versions of *Long Day's Journey into Night*, which is to say, I admired the performances of Katharine Hepburn in the film and Laurence Olivier in the TV version. At no time have I felt affection for the coy *Ah, Wilderness!* which in addition to the usual terrible O'Neill ear features the worst last line in theatrical history: "Yes, Nat." The echo as the curtain descends leaves one with the image of a gnat, perfect for the irritating and squashable effect of the play.

But here was a job and the Big Broadway Chance. Even gnats make singing noises. Several bookwriters were interested but the one that Merrick wanted, Sam Behrman, was not. He was then working on his own play of adolescent tensions, seduction, family conflict, *The Cold Wind and the Warm*, but I don't think the O'Neill play spoke to either side of Behrman's nature, one urbane drawing-room WASP, the other shtetl-roots Jewish. Behrman and his wife liked my music, and he praised the lyrics, but before our meeting was over he had alienated me by using one time too many the word *pansy*. *Daphnis et Chloé* was pansy music. So-and-So was a pansy designer. Thus-and-So had played a pansy Hamlet. Mr. Behrman looked like a plumber, which in fact a friend of mine mistook him for in a Deer Isle bathroom, and this, combined with a mind sometimes revealed to be delicate, brought irresistibly the image of the cartoon of a bruiser sniffing a violet. He was amusing on the subject of Max Beerbohm, provided you found the subject initially amusing—I never had—and seemed to extend a kind of shrewd-eyed sympathy in my direction. But we did not meet again for years. When we did he begged a favor which I refused. The favor was to stay on for the weekend in our mutual agent's house on Deer Isle, Maine, because he was bored to death with Harold and May Freedman, though he presented the boredom as that of his young secretary. My friend and I were on the way to the Gaspé peninsula and had only stopped for lunch and were reluctant to give the weekend to trying to understand what Harold was saying (he whispered). Behrman even ran after our car but—was this retaliation?—I said no.

Other bookwriters were eager to join the project but these were usually lyricists, and Merrick wanted my lyrics. For the phantom book I wrote ten songs which were played frequently at Merrick's hotel apartment, and sometimes at parties to which he would go if there was a hint of an angel in attendance.

At one such party in a chic East Seventies apartment I was giving the usual expository lead-in to the song as though there were in fact a musical book and was told by the aforementioned Alfred Katz, "Shut up, Jew boy, and play." This was rather more subtle than it sounds for what lay beneath it, since he liked the songs and intended to be the show's publicist, was regret at my not being Jewish. Once when things were going well he said, "If you were Jewish we could all lie back and rub our stomachs and qvell. But how can a goy kvell?"

Before my "career" in the theater was over I had been informed by a director that the New York theater had no need at all for non-Jews. I pass this along to Gentile and other —to Muslim and Buddhist and to atheist and Hindu, for he was a Very Big Director. He's dead now, but directing, one hopes, all-Jewish productions in an all-Jewish heaven. My own theatrical heaven would have resembled no doubt the Indianapolis project under Tyrone Guthrie—forever off-Broadway.

A Star-Bright Lie

Enter John Latouche, bookwriter, famous lyricist, and well-known goniff of other people's ideas. Or so I was told. "If you have an idea written under your balls, he'll find it." Ivan Obolensky told me that there was this awful little man . . . but talented. Latouche was a favorite of Obolensky's mother's. He was a favorite of many an aging and aged woman, few of them as charming as Alice Astor. There was Gilda Dahlberg, a gloomy woman encrusted like a Fabergé egg with jewels. There was Rozika Dolly of the once-feted Dolly Sisters, a George Grosz cartoon of a femme fatale, resembling more than a little, with her intricate exposed sinews and ligaments, some kind of instrument, but the sound that emerged from this instrument of leather and diamonds was the screech of a peacock. She would shout out such things as "my fifth husband for five minutes" and one wondered if she had had another fifth husband for, say, half an hour. But we were introducing John Latouche.

Some small creatures pull their smallness in around them, condensing themselves until it can be seen that they are presenting compactness as a means of disarming those around them. My terrier, when she wants to be picked up, offers her smallness as the best argument for the defense. A doorman whom I see each early morning just winding up his nightshift suggests that this small density on the other side of the glass door is the best reason his house should not be invaded; withdrawn into his greatcoat he shows a stubborn hopefulness in the kindness of strangers.

John Latouche, who could have qualified as a dwarf, was not this kind of small creature. His vast head belonged on a body six feet higher than his own, so that only seated in a passing automobile did he achieve his majesty—from the neck up, and swiftly transient. His ego could have outfitted

Coleman Dowell

a Sicilian village composed of Mafia chieftains. He was talented but perhaps not commensurate with his ideas of his worth. He had a bad temper and his determination to prevail matched that of the cockroach. He broke all the rules to cheat at games: "You mean you never heard of the twelfth-century Persian word for *shroff?*" This at a game of Scrabble with old ladies—Helvetia Perkins whom Jane Bowles immortalized (I do believe) and Louise Andrews Kent, Duchess of Kent's Corners. He pushed croquet balls with his feet and behaved outrageously at bridge. He was the perfect despot and at times incomparably good company, thus his allure.

He was signed on as book and lyric writer and we left with an entourage for his dreary house on the top of a mudhill in Vermont. Once there it became apparent that he had no intention of working on *Ah, Wilderness!* at all, which he referred to as a potboiler. By this he meant that the money Merrick gave him not to work kept the pot boiling while he worked on *The Ballad of Baby Doe* with Douglas Moore and *The Vamp* for Carol Channing. The parlors of Vermont were subjected to excerpts from the latter show. When inquiries were innocently made about songs from *Ah, Wilderness!* he would play them my song "Autumn," mangling the tune but letter-perfect on the lyric, for which he took the praise ... the lyric I had written for Lee Wiley and reworked for Aunt Lily in *Ah, Wilderness!* that was not to be heard on a stage until Carolyn Maye, as Lennie Colman, sang it in *The Tattooed Countess.*

As his parting advice Merrick had told me to do anything, by which he implied *anything,* to keep the temperamental Latouche content. The nuances were not so subtle but Latouche was happily well-fixed in that department, vide the entourage composed interchangeably, one noticed, of old and new lovers, male and female. Kenward Elmslie was there; Donald Fuller was there; a blond Mr. Martin was there; Ruth Landshoff Yorck (it was said that Brecht had written *The Jewish Wife* about her) was there, as was a small vivacious Indian woman whom Latouche said was a maharani but who herself said that that was only her name: Maya Rani. Latouche also introduced Ruth Yorck as Countess, for she had been married to a Count Yorck. . . . Why not Gräfin, in literate Vermont? But I can't fault him there, in this title-ridden book. Perhaps that most American thing, that shamefaced longing for a nobility tagged like trees wearing their Latin names, was my best bond with Latouche and should have been explored. To carry out Merrick's instructions I prepared and planted a garden, cooked, house-cleaned, picked up behind the imperial-mannered guests. I had only the living room to sleep in and, as Latouche stayed up until dawn, I was often sleepless. He would go up to bed at daybreak just as the others, healthy big boys and girls, were coming down expecting breakfast. I was two years older than the youngest of that crew, many years younger than the rest, but took on the role of parent, and scolded, and cleaned up after them, and sulked, and cooked good meals in the nice kitchen, thinking not so often anymore about the two-burner-cum-tin oven in the room I had shared with Kitty. When libido overcame I crawled into bed with someone and usually found a welcome. My lover was flying up to be met at Burlington each weekend. It was not an altogether bad time, but confusing: what to tell Merrick? Would it be obeying instructions not to report Latouche's duplicity (anything to keep him happy) or would I be called by Merrick a traitor? Guess.

Literary and theatrical figures came and went, as dinner guests, as house guests, or stayed nearby as summer or permanent residents. Norris Houghton of the Phoenix Theater was just down the hill in his pretty house which the sunlight could never touch; Mary McCarthy "moved like a cobra"— Latouche's imagery; I never saw her—up the hill and past the co-op store to and from her summer house; Harvard professors abounded. One's frumpiest neighbor trailing babies like a duckess possessed some arcane degree; conversation at square dances and yard sales could be incomprehensibly learned. We attended candlelit concerts in the Kent's Corners Tavern, sported in freezing blue water at a place called the Sliding Pools, a natural marvel hidden in deep woodland, fished, picnicked, made feasts in different houses, in the incomparable summer weather of northern Vermont. There were scandals, there were always fights at Latouche's. He was capable of the most blatant insults paid to company in company. He insulted his friends, his guests, me. My lover is a psychoanalyst and Latouche reserved his hatred for that profession (he had sent through the mail to his own analyst a box of shit) to those times when my friend (whom I shall call Allen) was there. My lover is also Jewish and Latouche insulted Jews continuously. It was not until long after his death, when a young man came to interview me about him, that I discovered his mother was Jewish.

Effie Mayer Latouche: I was told that Gore Vidal accused Latouche of hiring an old vaudeville actress to pose as his mother. She was either that, or one of the most innocent people alive. She was small, plump, disingenuous, full of appalling, unfunny Southern stories, and she was delightful. One of her poses, which may of course not have been a pose, was to ignore all signs pointing to her son's possible sexual "abnormality," as it was then called. Or that of her friends. Carson McCullers would dig, dig away, trying to make Effie

understand the relationship between her friends Helvetia
Perkins and Jane Bowles (their former relationship; Helvetia
at this time lived mysteriously in a handsome farmhouse in
Vermont, the house divided like a brain into the conscious
(downstairs) and unconscious (upstairs)): "Janie looked
across the street in Mexico and saw Helvetia and said, 'That's
for me!'" Effie would say, "How nice! People jest always
know who's goin to be their friend, right off!" One snowy
night in Manhattan Carol Channing, hugely pregnant, and
Axel Carson had to stay overnight and were put in the same
room—Miss Channing and Mr. Carson. At breakfast Carol
remarked that during the night her husband had said—and
Effie broke in, beatifically relieved, "You're *married!* How
nice!"

She and her son would fight fearsomely; he would back her
into a corner threatening mayhem, I would find them and
break it up, he would leave for New York—more frequently
as summer passed and the musical approached rehearsal—
and write to Effie what she described as "love lettahs—jest
exactly like a lettah from a lovah."

My lover and I and Effie spent two perfect weeks alone in
the cramped little house just prior to the onset of autumn.
The warm days turned cold at night so that one slept under
blankets. Effie made for us delectable Southern food and the
three of us around the table unselfconsciously made of our-
selves and our contentment a third entity, which was a happy
family. This was something no one of the three of us had ever
really known. She called us her sons. She had two of her own
but they hated each other and one love/hated her which
must have been a strain on little Effie Mayer Latouche, who
should have been a happy farmer's wife. She had to close her
eyes to too much, and of course to the fact that with enough

room now, my lover and I still continued to sleep together down past the pond in the screened-in one-bed house. But just now the thought presents itself that if we were her sons then there was nothing abnormal at all about our bunking together at the edge of the dark wood.

This pond house was one that Latouche said he had had built as a shrine, carefully aligned to sunrise-sunset, but which my lover and I had contaminated by sleeping in it rather than, the alternative, lying on the floor in the abysmally overcrowded bungalow. That day and night were a nadir, the end of the romance Effie and Allen and I had shared with nature. Latouche arrived from New York with several people, one of them Ruth Landshoff Yorck who exclaimed, "Mrs. Latouche has *my* room." Summer had revived for one day and the heat had brought on the flies and beckoned the mosquitoes, which did not help to calm those accustomed to self-indulgent displays of arrogance and temper. Effie wept but had no effective champion, and finally was taken in by Helvetia Perkins (a resigned, scarcely enthusiastic good samaritan). I refused to leave so late in the day—Vermont's motels back then were few and booked—and as someone was to have my old couch in the living room I took bedclothes and marched over the dam and made up a bed in the shrine. Ignoring Latouche's threatful protests seemed imperative. At one point he stood on the narrow dam and tried to push me into the black water. His remarkable eyes were devoid of sense, or of sensibility in the archaic meaning of receptiveness to our plight. I could have gone begging to neighbors and found a bed for Allen and me but why should I? The carload of spoiled and no doubt bone-weary sycophants had appeared without notice with Latouche, who had sent word, for there was no telephone, that he would be arriving sometime that week. Summer was ending, the only period of real creature comfort of the entire season plus half-a-spring for me; I had taken insults, had spent every penny of my advance money on the household, had labored, had lied to Merrick if only by omission, had slept like a slavey only when allowed. It was the end for Latouche and me and I told him so.

I have a photograph taken by Allen at my insistence (like an act of rape) the next morning. Latouche's eyes are still insane-appearing. He tried to detain Allen and me in spite of his rage, and I knew why: my departure would bring to an end the Merrick largesse. I wanted the photograph as a kind of record, for I knew I would never go back into that sterile relationship and probably that my Big Chance would be forfeit because of the decision. All I had was the evidence: my twenty melodies for *Ah, Wilderness!* and his two lyrics (the opening song and "Kissing Cousins," both charming); there was also his completed opera libretto and completed musical comedy. And Merrick had his own records, if he cared to consult them: the fifty dollars a week to me and the thousands to the great John Latouche.

Allen and I went to Maine and then home. There, all was as I had expected it to be. Latouche had seen Merrick and played him a series of songs composed apparently on the instant, songs said to be from our summer's long labors. Merrick had not been fooled and was horrified at what had become of my "Autumn" and another song he had particularly liked. Naturally he accused me bitterly of having been a traitor, of not reporting to him what had been going on. He had even heard from Latouche of my preference for gardening and cooking to writing music. I was let go, Latouche died before he could be fired, and Bob Merrill and another bookwriter were signed on for *Ah, Wilderness!* which became *Take Me*

Along and was a hit. I had been at work on casting and financing *The Tattooed Countess* when I read in the *New York Times*, while I was visiting in Louisville, that Merrick had signed my leading lady, Eileen Herlie, for his musical. The day before I left for Louisville, Eileen had called to praise exuberantly the new number I had written for her Countess, a habanera called "Continental Attitudes." She had not yet, however, been signed by my producers and expressed impatience during the same call. In my imagination I see her hanging up from the call with me and being called by Sam Zolotow about the rumor that Merrick wanted to sign her, and deciding in that instant, a mental toss of the coin, in favor of Aunt Lily over Ella Nattatorini. . . . I went to her opening night in New Haven, I kissed her in the dressing room, I congratulated Merrick; when *Take Me Along* opened in New York and was a hit, I gave a party for Eileen, a very successful, celebrity-ridden party. It was the last time I saw her. As for Merrick: in the heyday of our courtship, through no fault of his (you'll be glad to learn) a baby tooth of mine which had masqueraded for years, like me, as an adult, fell out; to fill the gap temporarily (a full-grown tooth lay horizontally in the gum and was brought down at the cost of a Broadway show through orthodontics years later) Merrick provided me with the money for a small detachable tooth. Blaming me for the fiasco of Latouche and *Ah, Wilderness!*, he told people, "I gave him a tooth and he bit me with it." Not then, David. Not then.

The Vamp failed but long before it did the rumors from Detroit of trouble and conflicts had set it up as that year's big flop (preceding *Butrio Square*, which some consider the worst musical of all time). Channing had Latouche barred from her dressing room and I think the director had him barred from the theater.

A Star-Bright Lie

The Ballad of Baby Doe was a success, a most beautiful and affecting production. The music has a nostalgic radiance and a technical perfection, for this was Douglas Moore's *Falstaff*. I find Latouche's lyrics for the songs, the arias, as simple and appropriate as can be though the sung dialogue is lazy, a compendium of clichés, a mistake I copied in my own *Tattooed Countess*. Not consciously. I would never emulate Latouche. For my approaching old age I sometimes pray for grace, for I am willful and bad-tempered, and believe "irascible" makes a dreadful pairing with "old." I also labor, sometimes very hard, to make accurate statements, to confine wishful thinking and fantasy to my novels and stories. Consider the words *aging liar*. They are not attractive, no more so than "irascible old" man.

John Latouche was not old when he died, but older than he, perhaps, thought. He maintained—not, of course, after death, at least I don't imagine so—that he was in his thirties. His bereaved mother, innocent as always, said that he was in his forties. I remember his dislike of his gray hairs and am able to feel some sympathy for his vanity. But not quite enough.

Not a year after the Vermont summer Latouche and the blond Mr. Martin were alone in the little house on the hill. Latouche suffered what I have heard was thought to be indigestion and he and Mr. Martin got out the medical book to look up his symptoms and a treatment for them. The pain going down the left arm, the erratic heartbeat, the other reported discomforts and irregularities comprised the syndrome of heart attack. But apparently Mr. Martin went into another room to sleep and Latouche—a telephone call away from salvation, perhaps, the telephone three miles down the road at the co-op store—died.

97

I was traveling in Europe with friends when a letter arrived for one of them telling of a séance in a house above the Hudson in which Mr. Martin's innocence (as it were) was established, for the medium announced "No foul play." I wanted to send a cable telling of a séance on the Palatine in which it was established through contact with Caesar that there was "no foul play" connected with his death, either. But was dissuaded. I suppose what I meant and mean was, wherever Latouche is, there is bound to be a certain amount of foul play. Perhaps this recountal comprises a bit of it. The facts are accurate, but *you mean you don't know the twentieth-century equivalent proper noun for Moloch?*

David Merrick, whose real name was Margolies, and I parted after the *Ah, Wilderness!* fiasco more or less in the following manner. He had often referred to me as the Golden Boy, unambiguous about what he meant: that I would make us both a fortune. I was the only melodist (his word at the time) among the younger crop who could hold his own with the Giants of Broadway Past. Therefore when the melodist sat before him, having been methodically broken into fifths, the great showman could not resist a final blow to the clavichord. He said to me, "Where will you go now, Golden Boy?" cold sarcasm his genius.

"Oh, I guess I'll move to Margolies, Long Island."

I won't explain the joke. (There's a Merrick, L.I.) He did not think I was funny.

B. C. and A.D.—after David and before Carlo—that would be Carl Van Vechten, whose *The Tattooed Countess* was to occupy the last years of my theatrical life—I fell into two traps. One could have produced valuable game in time; the other falling was an act of love, for which I was punished.

The potentially lucrative idea was to build a show around Stephen Foster's mind and music and tour it, for years if necessary, playing wherever we were allowed to, polishing the show and at last—though this was just a maybe—bringing it to an off-Broadway house in New York. This time I was signed as bookwriter and would do additional lyrics for which a classical composer would provide the music; he would also conduct the orchestra. This had been a brainstorm of Mr. Ross, whose first name I have willfully forgotten, though I believe he had found theretofore a niche in the theater. Ernestine Perry was to direct. Joe Moon was to do most of the musical labor. His crippled passion (he was one-legged) for the theater and his nearly total lack of acceptance by it made him a deeply poignant figure, more so now as I write. I've always appreciated deadlines and mine on *Beautiful Dreamer* was met with time to spare.

99

On the afternoon of the first reading aloud by actors I was told there had been a slight change in plans, and to be prepared to take it in stride. When we all arrived at Mr. Ross's apartment high up on Riverside Drive, before the reading of my rather pretentious but very literate play, we were given the "slight" change in plans: rather than the prolonged bus-and-truck tour—those years, remember, of polishing—we were to open cold in New York after the conventional rehearsal. Mr. Ross had even thoughtfully arranged for a theater. It was to be, after all, a commercial enterprise for which he felt we would all be grateful. And now without further ado let us hear Coleman Dowell's play.

Coleman Dowell's play had been tailored to specification, he had collaborated with the director on every page, and it would clearly not do at all; for college students, yes, certainly; for New York, no. Mr. Ross was deaf, dumb, blind to my accusations. Any work for the theater, whether college campuses (I swear he said "campi") or regional theater or New York, should keep in mind foremost that theater was the vox populi, which cried out in unison against words it could not say, such as—take page one of the play—"litmus paper." Paper, yes, but litmus? What the hell was that? And so on.

They gave me more money, I took it, then refused to work or to give back the money. I needed the money, I had been misled, my contract had been violated, and so sue me. They did not sue me.

William Engvick, who wrote the lyrics for the song "While We're Young," took over the job of playwright and kept as much of my work as he wanted—I recall one entire scene on a steamboat. The show flopped. It was small and dark and melancholy.

Following this I was asked to write music for a play called *The Crystal Tree*, an all-black show written by a white woman,

Doris Julian, who had been John Latouche's sometime secretary. She was a great beauty. She is dead but her children are living, at least one of them so harmed by life that I cannot add even symbolically to that harm, and so my lips, as they say, are sealed.

Doris had written the lyrics as well, and though I did not like them very much, they were at least rhythmic and the ideas were good, and for her lyrics and book I wrote the best, most complete and beautiful score of my life. The conductor, Sandy Matlowsky, went around telling people that I was the real thing, perhaps even another Gershwin. Helen Tamiris, who would choreograph the show, was enthusiastic about the rhythms though she admitted that her ear was made of purest tin. Perry Watkins, who would do the scenery and was himself black, thought the music was much truer to the black experience than any note of Gershwin's, and singers who might take part—among them a very young, ravishing Reri Grist, later of the Metropolitan Opera—were all enthusiastic about the songs that would be "theirs" in the show. Avon Long was pleased with the dance songs I had written for him, leaving musical space between the lyrics for some of his inimitable movements. Doris Julian was satisfied, I was euphoric. I had written my first complete score. Each character had his musical motif and these were woven into songs, dance music, connective tissue—a thorough, as we liked to say, integrated, score. No one ventured the word *hit* about what we were doing but all felt that our collaboration would demand, command, respect. That word was used a lot. We were now ready for auditions.

Enter Mr. Roger Stevens to the clank of money and fanfares of prestige, the only "incorruptible" man who ever produced a Broadway show, so the legend ran. Just preceding this time he had been on a roll and produced hit after hit, none of which I can recall. Research for the sake of the book would hurt me more than help me, for I came to hate the sound of "Stevens" so much that even my beloved Virginia Woolf suffered in my mind for her maiden name.

Told simply, Mr. Stevens's first premise was that the score for a show about blacks should be written by a black composer. Never mind Gershwin, never mind that the book of *The Crystal Tree* had been written by a woman as blonde as a Viking. Mr. Stevens, who endorsed the quota system, pushed before him like a tea cart laden with jam his integrity: he refused to hear a note of my score. I think that may have been not just a first, but an only. I was told that Avon Long presented my case to Mr. Stevens, the year of work, the musical understanding of the characters, the, to him, real success of my endeavors. Mr. Stevens's ears were clogged with his waxen integrity which only resembled, like the works of Madame Tussaud, real life, and that at a given distance. I would like to have discovered that he was a Quaker, for I have never known a Quaker nor a Buddhist who was not some kind of crook based on a phony integrity.

Here's what Mr. Stevens got for his money, rather a lot of it I was told: because he was a friend of Doris Julian's, Duke Ellington became briefly involved, but withdrew; two more black composers in fairly rapid succession appeared and either withdrew or were let go. I went, incorrigibly curious, to one Sutton Place audition of one of these black scores. It was okay but could hold no candle, not even a wick, to mine. The show faded from the columns, Mr. Stevens went off to handle other people's lives, Doris Julian wrote another play without music and found herself another Roger Stevens, this one Mr. Kermit Bloomgarden, and had her heart broken one time too many and died.

Some of the money Mr. Stevens was throwing around *The Crystal Tree* like a net to catch unwary birds came to me. Not enough. There was no such amount. But some. At my insistence, only. I had learned.

My final venture into other people's projects was when the aforementioned Joe Moon got me invited down to Philadelphia as a play doctor for a show in desperate trouble. This was *Portofino,* the logical successor to *Butrio Square,* some said. It had been written by Richard Ney of the movies, book and lyrics; one of the collaborators on the score was the jazz drummer Louis Bellson. I am ashamed to say that the other composer, an extraordinarily good and kind man, very talented, eludes me as to name and associations. Can this be because he was precisely so untheatrical, so steady, so unhysterical in face of so much of that theatrical commodity? After the show flopped he kept thinking of me and sent me jobs—I remember that at his recommendation I wrote some lyrics for a well-known harpist who fancied himself a balladeer. Perhaps this forgetfulness is another lesson learned in the theater: remember only those who are in a position to hurt you—which is another way of saying, bigger than you are.

Portofino starred George Guetary and Helen Gallagher, for both of whom the term "trouper" could have been invented. I went to Philadelphia through a heavy snowstorm, driving with Joe Moon, and arrived somehow in time for the Saturday matinee, and learned the extent of what I was up against. The show had one set, a bad book, lousy lyrics. Guetary and Gallagher were high-powered, sexy, charming, and someone named Strauss played the devil with such burlesque-comic verve and pushed so hard that the show almost made it out of the musty theater into the six-foot drifts, but here was a flop, the word writ large. Louis Bellson, whom I slightly knew, thought that the director (name forgotten) was at fault and suggested his own wife, Pearl Bailey, as the replacement. After the initial shock everyone was enthusiastic: if Pearl Bailey could not make something move and swing, who could!

I wrote all that night and all day and all of another night. As I wrote, the scenes were taken to the theater and rehearsed and put in. I was told that Gallagher and Guetary liked the new concept, which made the girl a shade neurotic: something to work with. Then it was suggested that I go on and rewrite the lyrics as well. Two nights and a day of work later, without sleep, I met Pearl Bailey just about dawn on the filthy Philadelphia street. She sat in the car with their adopted son, Jason, then a toddler, both of them swathed to the eyes in layers of clothing and Pearl Bailey in a vast fur coat. I stood in the snow and Bailey and I had the following exchange:

Bailey: "First thing to do [long hands waving] is to take that set, cut it in three parts and mount them on wagons so they can move. Then get some vendor's pushcarts out there—I don't care whether they have them or not in Portofino—and get some girls in bikinis, and some acrobats, and put them all to singing and dancing on those moving wagons, backwards and forwards, and you got the opening number. At least you've got some THEATAH."

Dowell: "Yes."

According to Louis, when I had gone up the snowy sooty street, his wife said, "If he stays on, I'll direct it."

I have not met Richard Ney. I am about to. At four o'clock in the morning, without sleep or food since I got to Philadelphia,

I find myself hanging out of the window of the Warwick, puking. Coincident with this the door knocks, a small pre-emptive warning, and in comes Richard Ney, dapper, fresh, uncannily calm, as remote from the cold and yet stuffy hotel room as summer and blue skies. He speaks little. I can't remember what he said. A while later we are sitting in a sort of diner eating petrified doughnuts, drinking some kind of barely warm liquid, so I must have confided in him my hunger and thirst. He talks, I nod. At one point my memory clears up as he says, "His head nodded and nodded like a bird drinking water." A comment upon me, my spastically agree-able head, my bird brain to be there at all? For I comprehend nothing. Soon afterward we are at the train station and I am boarding a train for New York. Again the clouds part and there he is, snowy as Annapurna, tall, his skin gleaming. "We'll be brothers," he says, "and have lunch together." The train moves out of the station. In New York I have to be literally knocked up, shaken, and pounded awake.

Pieced together, here is what happened.

Ney's wife, a very rich woman, had been either chief or sole backer and when everyone but Richard acknowledged that they were in deep trouble, she had caused papers to be drawn up stipulating that in return for continued backing her husband would stay away from the project, out of the theater, disentangled from the director's hair. Whoever came down to rework his material he was not to interfere with. And thus me and my isolation, the vacuum of that hotel room.

Then, the night of my meeting with Ney and departure, he had appeared, called the cast together, triumphantly announced that he had found a way to continue with *his* musical; and according to my multiple informants, with a quite dramatic flourish he drew a handkerchief from a bureau drawer, unfurled it, and a glittering mass of jewels tumbled out onto the bed. Some said a diamond bracelet, some said a necklace, some said both. I was of course not there. He came to me direct from his coup, shod with success, and gave me the boot. My gratitude to Richard Ney extends to this moment for I believe he gave me my life. I know I was sick with a bubbling in my chest that could have been pneumonia. The pills I had taken in quantity to stay awake worked a permanent change upon my body so that nearly thirty years later I cannot tolerate any kind of "up." That was one project for which I received no compensation except the paid hotel bill, and for which I asked none. I figured I had been more than amply paid in experience. I was followed by several other show doctors, as the personal fortunes of Richard Ney rose and fell with his wife's jewelry. I believe the last one, whose work actually came into the city limits of New York, was Sheldon Harnick. Though I was told that at the very last minute Ney demanded the reinstatement of all of his old material, the cast was thrown into a state of permanent confusion and demoralization, and the opening night of the show is considered by many as the reason nonpareil for why Mrs. Worthington should not put her daughter on the stage; or for that matter, any family member in any capacity whatever.

I had still two plays ahead of me, both mine, one without music, but I can see now (and feel in the reminiscently churning viscera) that my acute distaste for the claustrophobia within the confines of the theater, which extends even to too many of its members at one time, began with that puking episode at the Warwick Hotel. All the classic elements of theatrical narcissism and selfishness and perfidy are there, like rocks on the Portofino beach. (I went there, finally, along the twisting road, but could not bring myself to stay there and stayed instead at the Splendide-Hôtel in Santa Margharita, and remembered all night long my own *saison en enfer.*)

Years later, when I met Greer Garson, who was considering the role of the Countess, I told her that I had gone to Philadelphia as play doctor for her former husband's musical. Their marriage and the scandal of it had been a long time before, when she married the boy who had played her son in *Mrs. Miniver.* (The innocence of America then. Today as I write, a Miss America has caused much less flap by appearing naked in explicitly lesbian scenes in a dirty magazine.) Still, some of the trauma must have lingered for her, to make her say somewhat melodramatically but obviously with deep sincerity, "I *cannot* listen to anything to do with Richard. I *cannot.*" This most beautiful woman that I ever saw also told me, "I'm Irish, and will bring you luck, Mr. D." I sent her a rose with a stem so long that a box had to be specially made for it; the box cost more than the rose. To me, that could serve as a metaphor for most theatrical productions and for most theater people. But I won't belabor it for fear a thin trickle of sourness might be my only vintage.

Two theater people for whom I did feel affection at the time, and my memories of whom still give me pleasure, were George Kaufman and Leueen MacGrath. Their project, upon which I worked briefly, was then called *Love and War,* which became on Broadway *Silk Stockings.* This was, of course, the musical version of Garbo's old film, *Ninotchka.* The same Paul Bigelow who figured in the Tennessee Williams episodes recommended me to the Kaufmans and I went to see them in their penthouse at Eighty-sixth Street and Park Avenue. My coup for that day was making George Kaufman laugh. That I did it with a theft bothered me not at all. I had been presented

to the Kaufmans as Cole MacDowell, a name I had in fact
for a little while used, but I pretended that day that it was
all new to me, and said that it sounded "like somebody who
wrote 'To a Wild Beguine' " (this witticism was the property
of somebody in Louisville). Kaufman suggested that someday
there would be a statue in Gramercy Park to commemorate
my having lived there. It was an amiable meeting, I fell in
love with Leueen MacGrath, and George Kaufman made
me laugh by demonstrating his exercise regimen. He took
me onto their wraparound terrace and showed me a square
box, which could have been a cat's box, and said that he
walked around it every single day and looked at the distant
reservoir.

They casually asked me if I would like to write a song or
two for their book and I said I would. It clearly was not an
offer to collaborate with them, only an offer to show how I
would take to the material. I went home with the book and
within a week had written four songs. I had not told them that
the film was one I had seen a dozen times; their book was fairly
faithful and my songs, referring to the movie's ambiance,
served to fill in some emotional gaps in their own work. They
were generous in their praise. Kaufman said he had not heard
better lyrics since (the inevitable) Larry Hart's. Leueen liked
the tunes, and as I had done with the music for Avon Long, I
had left space between lines of lyrics for dancing. They
seemed definite in their wish to have me work with them; the
partnership needed only a contract, which would come from
Feuer and Martin, the producers.

In the meantime George Kaufman went to the hospital for
a prostate operation and Leueen and I spent a good deal of
time together, eating all the delicious things that people took
him to cheer him up—pâtés, caviar, marrons glacés. Then

one day came the news that the producers had signed Cole Porter. George Kaufman sent me a note of regret.

In the Cole Porter score there is a song called "It's a Chemical Reaction, That's All." In my partial score the song was called "Pavlov's Dog." The situation was the attempted seduction of Ninotchka by the hero. My cue was the remembrance of the way Ninotchka observed her would-be lover and said, "Your pupils are dilating." Here is the lyric, or what I can reconstruct of it. In those days I did not keep files.

Pavlov's Dog

By observing animals
Our scientists defined
The manifest and latent content
of the human mind,
And though the terms are slightly
euphemistic
The symptoms you display
Are merely an intensification
of a universal characteristic.

The theories are similar
And most of them enrich
From Kamichev and Pavlov
Jung and Adler
down to Kinsey-vorovitch.
One experiment in particular
Did much to lift the fog:
Take the case of Pavlov's dog:

Comrade Pavlov
Had a theory
And a dog named Ned
And to make his

109

Coleman Dowell

Theory clear he
Cut off Neddie's head.
Though Ned couldn't wag his tail
He was reported doing well
He ate and ate
And theoretically grew

Pavlov thereby
Proved that sex is
Quite without a doubt
Just a series
Of reflexes
We can do without:
Pavlov's dog existed years with
Nothing much to scratch his ears with
And his other parts
Were equally few.

[*second verse*]

Pavlov states
That thought expended
On erotic whims
Brings a lethargy
Extended
To the lower limbs,
Pupils may become dilated
And the pulse exaggerated
Symptoms which are difficult to subdue

Human moral fiber
lessens
And may even die
Through repeated
Acquiesence
To some stimuli,

A Star-Bright Lie

Pavlov's dog
aesthetically
Retarded, and it's
said that he
Discarded any other comfort
But stew.

[*section missing here*]

Comrade Pavlov
Then grew weary
Of his canine's head
And resolved to
Try his theory
On himself, instead

[*Kisses, Ninotchka weakens*]

Though it's painful
to relate it
Comrade Pavlov
Illustrated
Just the opposite of what he descried

[*She gives in*]

And Comrade Pavlov died.

Soon after this someone gave me a copy of a novel, *The Tattooed Countess,* and for the next six years I was to labor like the mountain which gave birth to a mouse, but when it was first completed "everyone" wanted to play *my* Countess, about which Fania Marinoff said to her husband, Carl Van Vechten, the author of the novel, "You wrote a silly woman and Cole has written a witty one." "Everyone" who wanted to play her included Margaret Leighton, Eileen Herlie, Greer Garson, Gail Manners, Ethel Colt Barrymore. David Merrick (yes, the same one) wanted to interest Mary Martin, upon whose approval his producership devolved. I told Harold Freedman, my agent and the one who brought Merrick back into le tableau, "I'd rather be crippled all at once than in slow stages." But Merrick was by then Broadway's Innovator, its towering flagship, and whether loimous or not, the locks had to be opened when he wanted passage. I'm happy to say that Mary Martin took on *The Sound of Music* about then, and Merrick withdrew his tentative interest.

I was in Easthampton for a weekend when a call came from Freedman, late on a Saturday night, asking me to return the next morning to play the songs for another of B.way's hot-shots. This red-haired man is still producing movies and is, I'm told, litigious, so I will not name him. But I made the journey in, Freedman and his wife pointedly left us alone by leaving the apartment, Harold saying to me, "It's all up to you now" with a curious inflection, and the producer lost no time in making his pitch, both for the musical and for me. The only catch was, he wanted me first. I suggested that he fuck himself instead, thereby earning not only his enmity but, as it turned out, that of my agent, who incidentally was a pious Jew who kept a kosher household. I suppose there are kosher pimps.

I have jumped far ahead. The first part of this book to be published, publication happening along about the time that I write these words, was/is the section devoted to Carl Van Vechten and his remarkable salon, to which I was afforded entry by my musical *The Tattooed Countess*. I will present it here pretty much as published, as a set piece, in *Bomb* magazine, in the autumn/winter issue of 1984.

At Home with Drosselmeyer

My first impression of Carl Van Vechten's drawing room was the lasting one. The day of our meeting in January 1957 was dark and the chandelier was blazing. Coruscant in its light were sea green *peau de soie*, china cats, portraits, the marzipan colors of Impressionist paintings; on a large table under the source of light were boxes: of silver, cloisonné, sandalwood, studded with turquoise or lapis lazuli, or intricately inlaid. Later I was to be offered from those boxes candied ginger, crystallized violets and rosebuds, and other sweetmeats to rival the delights of Confiturembourg in *The Nutcracker*. If Fritz rather than Clara had been bewitched by Herr Drosselmeyer and taken out of this world, the analogy to the changes wrought in my life for a time would be exact. Van Vechten was a master magician and some of his illusions over the years were disquieting.

He was an original man, but his greatest asset was to have been "of his own time," a more primary guarantee of temporal success than great originality.

The reason for our meeting was that I might try to persuade him to allow me to turn his 1920s novel *The Tattooed Countess* into a musical. I went there knowing that others had been

113

refused the rights, some of them Great Names—Richard Rodgers among them; but I was in my twenties and somewhat arrogant, arrogant enough to have written a great many songs and several dialogue scenes before I asked permission of him. Before I played the music for him he assured me that our "contact" (his amused word) had guaranteed my talent, and he was happy for me; but Hollywood had made such a mess of the movie version, called *Woman of the World* and starring Pola Negri, that he had sworn off allowing any further adaptations of his works. Still, I was not intimidated, and the songs hooked him, and I left with his approval and permission. A letter from him a few days after our meeting is full of his enthusiasm. By that time I had been—commanded, I suppose is the best word—to show up and be photographed, and another early letter tells me that the first batch of proofs is highly successful, adding that he does not know, however, the way people like to see themselves.

A letter not too long after that bids me show up with my lion, which was stuffed, unlike Tallulah Bankhead's which, in one photograph, is in the process of scratching her badly; it is in color and the drops of blood are like small jewels strung on the long pink chains of the scratches. That was just pre-zoo for the lion of Tallu.

In the letter concerning my lion, perversely named Tiger, Van Vechten says that the three of us must be photographed by his assistant for posterity, ". . . while I am still alive and you are still beautiful."

Looking over the letters for the first time in years, I am amazed at how quickly I was drawn into that circle; made, in fact, the often unwitting center of it. One letter, about a party that I did not attend, brings this home: "Despite the mention of Langston's name the party was for you and arranged around you." (That would be Langston Hughes, an intimate friend of the Van Vechtens and a remarkably sympathetic man.) I am pleased to see that I at least sent flowers, for he mentions that they have been photographed "so they exist in perpetuity!"

If one great comparison is more apt than another I would say that the Louvre under Louis XIII best presents the atmosphere of Carlo's drawing room. There was a measure of rivalry and envy perhaps a little greater than is usual in New York circles, but it was also more submerged; all the unsavory implications and directives, there, fell through the interstices of ordinary speech, so ordinary as to be surprising, at first: one had expected elevated talk of the great, and high bitchery, and found instead banalities, imagined until then to have been the special province of the Midwest. (I had, of course, taken my ideas from Van Vechten's own novel, and finally it was enough to know that he had been capable of writing it.) The games hidden beneath this mundane surface could be quite cruel but one knew it only after one had been for the first time badly wounded. My first time occurred on an evening when the press of the famous had made me a wreck at the thought of playing my *Countess* songs, a feature of most gatherings at Carlo's in those early years. Leontyne Price sang, Geoffrey Holder improvised a dance, his long fluttering hands like big tropical butterflies, and a pianist just launching a concert career played something brilliant and showy. When it came my turn I refused. Gloria Vanderbilt and Sidney Lumet, then Mr. and Mrs., insisted that I play; they had not heard the songs and would not tolerate my refusal (this said so very nicely, Mrs. Lumet's eyes crinkled persuasively). Thus won, I went to the piano and played an introductory chord, and the Lumets left. Instantly. The game perceived, I sat on and played the songs and sang them, and my champion was Langston Hughes. There are compensations for the victim of such games: I have never played so many encores on request.

I wonder if it would amuse the altruistic originator of Fat Lady Jeans, the former Mrs. Lumet, to learn that her nickname among us was Ears? One was fascinated by their size and prominence, as one still is, and by her skin so fine-grained but dead white and as exhausted-looking as a Southern lady's handkerchief in a 1930s August.

Leaving Mr. and Mrs. Lumet now, I allude to a discussion which will give a sense of the importance of talk at Van Vechten's: a discussion about big ears on women; it was said that their size connoted the dimensions of her sex, which led to more bawdiness concerning the penis sizes of the lovers of these jug-eared women. This improvisation was prolonged because Carlo was so amused by it, and fell from the sofa onto the floor suffering all the visual symptoms of apoplexy. The old queens impassively watched one's efforts to turn the massive body which once turned was subjected to an extremely amateur mouth-to-mouth resuscitation. Dead silence and then wild laughter as Carlo's tongue shot into my mouth, the moment for which he and they had been waiting. They knew their man.

Often the evenings were spent innocently, writhing on the floor in laughter at Florence Foster Jenkins; or less innocently refraining from laughter at Paul Swan's dance recitals where dancer and audience practiced an extreme form of masochism. The Gish sisters were visitors there, and the most regular of regulars was the silent-film actress Aileen Pringle. Her irreverence touched everyone and her tales of early Hollywood could be chilling as well as funny. If I've got it right, she was the daughter of a governor of Bermuda and had some claim to a feeling of superiority to what she called "mostly trash," that is, the early screen stars. She was definitive on the subject of William Randolph Hearst and Marion Davies, the latter her "pal"; I wish I could set it all down here, her recountals of evenings at San Simeon, but I am afraid I might find that I had violated somebody's trust—perhaps Pringle's if she is still alive. She was rather tender about Elinor Glyn, which was refreshing; and chilling about Van Vechten's Hollywood days. "He taught us," she said, "to accept niggers." This was in Nora Holt's apartment in Harlem with Jimmy Daniels and other blacks in close proximity. I've discovered that no word carries farther in a stage whisper than *nigger*. But I suppose they had all been through it together before, for they were old friends linked by what seemed a genuine affection.

Another silent-film star habituée was Dagmar Godowsky, who liked to sit near to and facing the door; she explained this in a Viennese accent so thick it was more like a hearty soup than speech: "I'm a snob. I like to sit where I can see who is arriving." I gave one party, at least, that met her standards; there were movie and stage stars, a political figure, one clothes designer of-the-moment and a beautiful model, and three English ladyships, all oversized, perched like big, not-too-friendly birds on the only old, fragile piece of furniture I owned, a seventeenth-century refectory table. This was either a party for Eileen Herlie, whom we were courting to be our Countess, or it was in honor of a Van Vechten anniversary. For all my total recall I cannot somehow separate those two occasions, but if it was the latter then Carlo was responsible for the guest list and I believe the ladyships came with Hermione Baddeley, one of my friends. Anyway, Dagmar approved of everything, even the uninvited guests who made us run out of food ("People should not eat too much in public"—a revealing statement; Daggie was very fat). The last time I saw her she bade me come by and meet her monkey. I'm sorry I never went.

Thus the circles, Carlo's and mine, became interchangeable. He photographed my friends and nourished them on bad gumbo and good champagne; I fed and bourboned his friends and stored up mental portraits. The parties back and forth across the Park grew so incessant for a time that I pretended to always be busy on Thursdays so I could get some rest, but after tasting Sardi's Thursday special, osso buco, I again became available, for Van Vechten was almost always in that place, and thus we began to go together. I tried asking Vincent Sardi to keep his waiters from standing around watching Carlo eat. I said it was like feeding time at the zoo, meaning the waiters' horrified attention, but Sardi turned it against me: "You should not say such things about your friend." I would tuck Carlo's napkin about him, tie it around his neck, but food still spilled and gravy still ran and often shot between his teeth in trajectories that could score bull's-eyes on the waiters. But the wonder was that Carlo's widely spaced, exceedingly protuberant teeth could retain anything at all. Still, a provincial myself, I would sit there loathing the waiters whom I saw as newly arrived from Sicily, saying to myself, "He's old, world-famous, does everything with gusto, and it doesn't matter what people think about him, especially waiters." But it mattered to me.

A letter of January 3, 1958, informs me that there will be an informal supper party for the Baroness Blixen ("of Denmark," he writes, perhaps fearful for my literacy) "on Sunday evening at six o'clock." It appeared that the Baroness wished to meet some American Negroes, and so would I come?—a typical Van Vechten dig at the young white Southerner. . . . It occurs to me just at this moment that perhaps Pringle's use of the word *nigger* was somehow meant to discredit me, and that they were all in on it—Jimmy Daniels, who was definitely not my friend, and Nora Holt, who was. . . . If this is paranoia it is not the first nor will it be the last instance, though I believe this mild affliction began at Van Vechten's where it could have been designated, like the pox at older courts, the Court Disease.

One's intuition, of which paranoia may be a legitimate appendage, could become extraordinarily sharpened by contact with the crowd at Van Vechten's. I generally arrived at his house after several drinks at home but on that Sunday I stayed on the wagon. When I arrived at 146 Central Park West I was sober, and apprehensive. The drawing room was unusually packed, people ranged around the walls in layers. At each new arrival everyone craned, expecting the great writer. I wondered if they all held her in the same veneration I reserved for her exclusively; she and Edith Sitwell were the only literary figures for whom I had ever felt awe, one for her great discipline, the other for her lack of restraint; but to me Isak Dinesen stood on a pinnacle that the great Jacobean poseur could never have attained. . . . The bending human walls at each ring of the doorbell seemed about to permanently cave in, so that to one's apprehension was added acute claustrophobia, and the curtains in that drawing room were never opened, not even during the day, so that one was caught forever in the chandelier's blaze.

I wonder if it was intuition that informed Carlo, for he answered one ring of the door himself. In a funereal quiet—little coughs, a few shuffles of the feet—he escorted Isak

Dinesen to her thronelike chair. She was dressed in black—silk jersey, I think—and wore a large black hat deeply edged with plumes. As they progressed, she leaning upon him, half his height and a quarter his weight, the black plumes funereally nodded, now this side, now that, but we could not see her face. When she had been seated and given champagne Carlo turned about and surveyed the room, head lowered as though he peered over the tops of glasses. My heart failed when his eyes stayed on me. "Cole," he said, "come and talk to the Baroness." I sank to my knees before her, a graceful gesture, but it was because I could not stand.

I spoke to her of our joy at having her in America, her first visit. She spoke. I spoke. And spoke. "I will accept as many invitations as I can," she told the room in reply to my invitation to dinner. Was it a bid for rescue? In desperation I told her that I had read recently a book by a fellow countryman of hers, and though it would be second-rate Isak Dinesen I thought it was first-rate anybody else: *The Red Umbrellas,* by Kelvin Lindemann.

For the first time the plumed hat brim was tossed upward, a movement of great abruptness, and the fascinating face was revealed. But the eyes, surely, were blazing in anger? They were. She said that the book had been submitted and sold under her name, a fact well known in Denmark but unmentioned in the reviews in this country. Her rage, larger than our context of the drawing room, greater than the company, was focused upon me. What an awful thing it had been for her, that deception! She can only have believed that I knew of the controversy which involved a lawsuit, and had baited her deliberately.

Was the shifting about behind me of all those bodies sympathetic to my plight or impelled by a peculiarly New

York glee? As for me, I discovered in myself a potent dislike for the Baroness Blixen; in fact, I detested her with all my humiliated spirit, attaching my loathing like a leech to her titled self, which left Isak Dinesen, the revered, in the clear. My bestowal upon her of this schizophrenia—which may in fact have afflicted her in her daily existence—allowed the denouement of this episode and permits me to tell it now, though not without shame.

Our encounter ended with Donald Gallup's rush to the rescue and I melted into the murmuring and certainly malicious crowd: all contact with me was avoided. From this vantage point of twenty-six years later I view all of us with a certain compassion. We were playing the game as we had been taught, abiding by stringent rules that were tarnished heirlooms by the time we received them from an older, more ruthless race—see James and Wharton—and from a time when certain concepts, such as society and honor, had almost totally different consequences, if not meanings. Whether or not the motivationless malice of much of today's sport is better I can't say, but suspect that structured, official, mandated cruelty is more regrettable, as malice aforethought is more deplorable than a spontaneous act of similar weight.

To return to one's story: a feature, a phoenix far too frequent, of Carlo's parties was a woman of such monumental ability to bore that she was surely a genius. I cannot characterize her further, for she is still alive. Except to say that her one claim to distinction was her marriage to a black man; one so far Right that some called him a fascist, but, you do understand, black.

Leashed by my powerful intuition I was drawn from the supper table and down the corridor to the drawing room door, where I was allowed to lean and observe. At the other

121

end of the vista, tiny and shocked, sat the Baroness in the clutches of you-don't-know-who. Untouched before her were oysters and champagne, and a peanut butter canapé appeared to be stuck to her long black glove; she would extend her hand in slow motion toward a dish as though to part with the canapé but when her hand again lifted the Ritz cracker was still with her; this maneuver, performed two or three times while I watched, led to the conclusion that she was involved simultaneously in a Bea Lillie comedy and, with the jawing Lorelei, a tragedy. Observing the perpetual motion of the jaw of Mrs. S. I could imagine what she was saying. If you had been on an automotive journey with that woman she would have gone something like this: "Here comes a telephone pole; it's getting closer; now it's passing; now it's gone. And *here* comes *another* telephone pole. . . ." All the way from New York to California.

The rest of the story is simple. The black plumes once again lifted, the great haunted eyes met mine across the centuries of boredom, and forgave, and beseeched. And I went away. If there is a chamber for me in hell, Mrs. S. will join me there and tell me, forever and ever, what she was saying to Isak Dinesen, for I became convinced it was she and not the cruel Baroness who begged for my help.

At large parties tables were set up in the library and in Carlo's studio. The library could accommodate at least a dozen people and was where the fun was. The studio contained only two tables, four people to each. I had the thought that those in the studio were isolated as people with diseases are, to see how they will infect each other and respond to stimuli and certain medicines. Once I was put in there with Brooks Atkinson, Ruth Ford, and Irene Dalis of the Metropolitan

Opera, a memorable Fricka. I had never seen Miss Ford act, and Atkinson, for all his milquetoast appearance, inspired fear. At the other table sat Louis Kronenberger, also a critic.

Ruth Ford—none of us had met Atkinson before—attacked at once. Atkinson apparently had given her a bad notice for something years ago, perhaps for her Temple Drake in *Requiem for a Nun*. She informed him, in her somewhat harsh voice, that his duty was to her, not the other way around; that he should make every effort to understand what she was doing, and that she should not ever have to worry about what *he* was doing. And the *Times* critic agreed. And agreed. Occasionally Miss Dalis would interject something about her roles in Wagner but Miss Ford did not care and Mr. Atkinson could not, or maybe he did not want to, break the spell. Miss Ford was extremely handsome in her indignation, the slight Southern cast of her speech both charming and threatening, in the way that a cast in the eye can convey beauty or a malediction.

Carlo and Fania Marinoff, his wife, wandered through the rooms with magnums of champagne; visiting the tables, as he filled our glasses she hung from his shoulder in her ancient and beautiful clothes (she swore that she had not bought a new dress since the 1920s) that were like tapestries, or rugs. Their orbit resembled a comet's and I came to wish that they were Halley's which appears only every seventy years or so. Because each time they got to us Fania would shout, in her rich, actressy voice, "Brooks, remember that name: COLE-MAN DOWELL." And I could feel Mr. Kronenberger turning behind me, perhaps metamorphosing into the monster of, was it *Time* magazine? In any case, the monster of opening nights. After several of these mad ellipses my prayer was that before my opening night something would have wiped the occasion from their minds. As it turned out by then Atkinson had retired and had been succeeded by someone who had the shortest term of any "critic" in history, and Kronenberger, if he was still around, did not bother to review the musical, for which I was grateful.

There is no denouement to this story. Unlike "Mare" Koch (as the newscasters call him) I was seldom victorious and all my enemies went, and go, unscathed. No, like most parties, that one was not rounded off but remained open-ended, all things possible as the result of friendships and animosities engendered there. For all Van Vechten's Drosselmeyer-like magical abilities, he could not influence the future beyond arranging meetings, which you and I can do, and laying plans which, for all their intriguing elaborateness, ganged aft a-gley. This was a disappointment to me, that the old, very famous and accomplished man could not, for example, order a theatrical hit, or good reviews, or force two people to fall in love. Though he did mate them, or cause them to mate.

When Leontyne Price came to him, from Mississippi—as so many black artists came from all over the country for his evaluation, assistance, aegis in cold, hard, anti-black New York—he told her he had just the husband for her and introduced her to William Warfield, and they got married. Whether one says "dutifully" I can't tell you. The marriage did end in divorce, but they were still married when I knew them up at Carlo's.

However, there was a small and at the time funny consequence of my meeting that evening the actress Claudia McNeil, one of the stars of *Raisin in the Sun.* We liked each other and spent the rest of that evening together, but that seemed to be the end of it, for months went by and neither of us called the other. Then we met again at a luncheon at Le

Moal, the host of which was of course Van Vechten. It was a large and "famous" crowd and the table had been carefully arranged to accommodate our ambitions for *The Countess:* we finally had producers and a tentative star in Eileen Herlie, my first choice. On one side of my place card was Al Hirschfeld's, which was meant to guarantee that our show, no matter what else was opening in the same week, would dominate through the Hirschfeld drawing on the front page of the theater section on Sunday before our first night. Carlo arranged the table; I was to see to the rest. On the other side of my place card was Danton Walker's, who actually gave me a tiny plug in his column the following week. But not because I had through proximity and charm influenced him: Claudia, who always referred to herself in the third person—Claudia thinks, Claudia feels, Claudia does—thought we should sit together, *felt* we should sit together, and Claudia *did*—she rearranged the table to her satisfaction. Carlo watched help-lessly; perhaps he was amused, perhaps he approved, for he admired chutzpah above all other attributes for which no word exists in English.

It occurs now, struggling with this memory, that Claudia McNeil's officious friendliness may have shifted the bobbins of a few fatal threads, helping to alter the pattern from what would have been into what came to be. Why else the occa-sion, the occurrence? For I never saw her again and yet I see now that that day marked a change. . . . But hindsight, like lupus, is the great pretender: remove one of its masks and another lies beneath, just as convincing. . . .

Also at that luncheon was Mattiwilda Dobbs, who sang, during my Van Vechten years, what he termed the only perfect recital he had heard since—was it one of Mary Garden's? Anyhow, that other "perfect" recital had been a hell of a long time before. Miss Dobbs was very beautiful and as remote as, for example, Leontyne Price seemed to be accessible. But this latter star concealed another star within, and the sharp points were not aligned. . . .

Among the people I took as gifts to the Van Vechtens were Kim Hunter and Bob Emmett, Tamara Geva, Balcomb Greene and his wife Terry, and Ruth Yorck. Carlo *knew something about Ruth Yorck* but would not say what it was. In my presence they had a cryptic exchange in which the name Josephine appeared regularly, and the smiles were like a game, bold, elusive, as they took turns pursuing and eluding and implying. This was what passed for conversation at Carlo's; in all the years I spent in that place I never heard nor took part in a conversation as I define the word; at Carlo's there were monologues, exchanges of bon mots, bitchery, some facts, but there was never the give-and-take of conversation. Years later, many years later, I discovered what I think it was that Carlo knew and Countess Yorck knew he knew about her: in the biography of Josephine Baker there is an anecdote in which Miss Baker and a woman "named Landshoff"— Ruth's maiden name—are depicted as being naked at a party of men, barons and the like, in Germany. They fall to kissing each other, then fall, or sink, to the floor for more serious embracing, and the men gather round for the show. . . . Someone who had known Ruth in Germany had said, "She was the most exciting woman in Berlin at that time," and when I pressed him for reasons all he could come up with was that she had ridden her motorcycle into the opera house. But clearly her fame amounted to more than that, and what Carlo knew was simply this sexual license of which I was perfectly aware. What candor am I allowed? These are memoirs, not

fiction. Having reminded myself of this I replay an old sound-
less memory of Ruth coming out of the bathroom at John
Latouche's in Vermont followed by an embarrassed (and
obviously gay) black pianist then studying in a nearby village;
Ruth is lustily wiping her mouth. A successful encounter,
later verified by the pianist to his friends, though he got the
title of the fellator wrong: he told them "the duchess" had
done it. And here is Ruth talking of the pleasure of playing
with a lover's feces, a word she would never have used. Shit
it is and shit it was. The last time I saw her was at her tiny
house on Cornelia Street, in the garden strung with Japanese
lanterns, the garden packed with people among whom were
a name or two—Marguerite Young comes to mind—the
purpose of the gathering being that all whom she had helped
in their careers should be photographed in motion for German
television. I had just begun my third career, as a prose writer
(simultaneous with my second career as a model) and Ruth
had translated and seen into publication in Germany a story
of mine, and this is why I was there. I can't recall why it was
the last time we saw each other; there was esteem between
us; I think our estrangement was on account of a letter I published in the *Times* in support of a Professor Poll of Columbia
whom Leo Lerman had typically attacked, gnat stings all over
the poor professor's body. I've always, as a Southerner should,
detested gnats. Ruth, I recall, was unaccountably fond of
Lerman and when I threatened on the telephone (to her) to
follow up my letter with a physical attack on him she told me,
in vibrating cello tones, how delicate the person was compared to me, and contrasted our ages, and asked me to feel
"just a little ashamed, my darling." I didn't and somehow that
may have brought our physical encounters to an end, though
we still spoke on the telephone. Is it a faulty memory that lets

me recall plans we had made to go to Vermont, to Latouche's house (Latouche then dead, Kenward Elmslie the squire of the tiny house) just before she died at a matinee of *Marat/ Sade* in Ellen Stewart's arms? I know we had such plans once, and that they were frustrated, and I choose now to think that only death . . . you know. But it was probably something petty on my part. "My Greek boy" she called me. I never knew why.

Carlo always *knew something* about everyone, which he was determined to keep from me. When I asked, for example, just what Gertrude Stein meant about Hemingway's muttering that he could not tell all because of his public, he looked enigmatic and even censorious, and clammed up, though he was also master of the seeming non sequitur when he said, immediately afterward, that Gertrude would have loved me. He called out to Fania to verify the statement and she did. "What do you *mean? Why* would she have loved me?" No answer. And in my emphatic questions (emphases my undoing?) perhaps they heard the child, and you do not tell things to children. Though unprodded he did tell me—with such seriousness—that Alice Toklas was "the man." Years later there was a slight world ripple at the revelation that the two women had been lovers: as Carlo would have said, for God's sake!

Did I carry Barbra Streisand to him? I hope so, for they belonged together: his camera and her photogenic face, his piano and her voice, his approving eyes (and Fania's) and her thrift-shop clothes which looked very much like Fania's own rugs and tapestries. And of course there would have been her Jewishness and his approval. Next to blacks he felt most passion for Jews. (Fania, announcing to the world in her stentorian voice, "I'm a *Jewess,* darlings.")

A Star-Bright Lie

I carried a lot of young men to Carlo, either because of their beauty and/or eccentricity, or because they practiced some offbeat hobby or profession, such as deciphering hieroglyphics, or because they were Jewish. I met Peter Feibleman at Carlo's and he managed to combine all the above elements and attributes. He had just published a very eccentric and lovely novel, *A Place without Twilight*, he was an American Jew, and he had lived in Spain and acted upon the Spanish stage as a Spaniard, without detection, when such a masquerade was extremely dangerous. Or so the story ran. I also met James Purdy there, God knows talented, God knows eccentric; and God surely knows, *not* Jewish. I have never met a more perfect embodiment of Middle America, nor of Waspishness. In a letter to me after Van Vechten's death Purdy says that he does not believe Carlo loved him. But the letters I have from Carlo about Purdy refute this, and he cautions me to keep Purdy's letters as long as I like but that they must eventually go to the collection at Yale. Purdy was touched with magic for me even before I read his stories (he had not yet written one of his odd novels) because Edith Sitwell herself, great authoress of *Facade* and *The Canticle of the Rose*, had been his champion, had called him "an American genius." Hearing of this before our meeting I prepared myself for nuances, for an offbeat beauty, a sense of turbans and pearls. But found the uncompromising bleakness of his own "Daddy Wolf." And a certain defensiveness about his work that could easily pass as pettiness. Referring to a story of his, in which a mistreated child spews something black from his mouth, I asked the author "*How* could you do it?" and won, I think, his enmity which, through our sporadic letter-writing, was never far below the surface. Recently someone I know went to interview Purdy, all the way to Brooklyn and the one room I had heard about but never seen, and I sent regards. According to my informant the only response was "He hates my writing." I had never thought about it until then.

Two black women refused to let me take them to Van Vechten's, both of them for the same reason: they had been warned by their parents against being drawn into the racist, and worse, web. One of the women, Barbara Scott Preiskel, had been given the warning in Washington; the other, Lorraine Broyard, had received instruction in Sag Harbor. When I cruelly (I later saw) tricked Barbara by inviting her to a party with Van Vechten she chose the alternative to meeting him, which was to leave. I suppose I had not realized the depth of her conviction, nor the breadth of his specific reputation. Several years ago she was listed among the ten most successful women executives in America, one black at least who succeeded without Van Vechten intervention! Lorraine Broyard's claim on my memory is two-pronged. The first horn of the dilemma, as I see it, is that she refused to sleep with me because I was too old; I was still clinging to my twenties at the time. The second horn is that her brother, to whom she showed my first stories, sent strong encouragement, saying to her, "Your friend has something," but now I wonder what it was he meant that I had, for in his capacity as a book reviewer for the *Times* he has never paid notice to my "mature" writing. Still, Anatole, thanks for the early kindness and if your sister is still around, kiss her for me and tell her that I am really too old now.

Entr'acte

Others one saw with regularity at the San Remo on Central Park West were Diahann Carroll whose beauty, like Miss Dobbs's concert, seemed to me to be perfect; Nora Holt, upon whom Van Vechten had patterned the siren in *Nigger Heaven;* she had once, it was said, been truly wicked like Lasca in that novel but was now (then) a cultural leader in a Harlem beginning to break out of its Northern bounds and move South; and there were the Lin Yutangs. If a softening of tone is discernable it is meant to be, for this lovely philosopher and his family always had that effect upon me. They arrived always in the spirit of Christmas, their voices beyond doors like bells, their hands bringing charming gifts. Chinese Baptists!, somehow risible; but they were still very Chinese. We discovered that we lived in the same building and as friendship advanced we made feasts for each other which did not have to include the Van Vechtens. Madame Lin invariably put me on her right and I'm fairly sure this was because I drank so much and each time she poured wine for me she could pour for herself, and she would urge me, "Drink up, drink up!" She was allowed by Dr. Lin two martinis before dinner and wine with but nothing afterward, and both attitudes were informed by her having had a heart attack in the recent past.

In my bookshelves I have a copy of Dr. Lin's *Imperial Peking* inscribed to me on my birthday, May 29th, 1962, and this helps recall the birthday feast and the dish named in my honor, Crystal Shrimp (I was at work on a new musical with "crystal" in the title). I loved Dr. Lin's serious consideration of all things—a pipe in mouth seriously contemplating the little plastic recirculating fountain in my living room—and

Hong's apparent giddiness, and the beauty of Mei Mei, and the endearing sobriety, like a child's, of Adet, who, like her father, was a brain; and I loved their options: Shall we, they would ask, move to Paris, or Taiwan? When his plane would land in such as Brazil or Argentina, hordes of teenage fans would be there to greet him. Try to imagine philosopher-groupies in our own country.

We did not see very much of Alicia Markova but when she was in town there was always a celebration. Her beauty and the unequaled grace of her walk turned us all into quietened spectators. Once when I was in London I was taken to tea with her sisters, Doris Barry and Vivian Marks. The apartment was a shrine to Markova; ballet slippers were framed like paintings. They referred to their sister as madame and there was perceptible neurosis in their talk of her, though the talk was not reluctant. This eager neurosis intrigued me. When I saw Markova again I told her of the visit. This did not please her at all. Was it because the London apartment was decidedly shabby and might with its pervasive comfortable ordinariness spoil the gossamer she had woven from her own body into an aura over the long years? It's true that one imagines a Markova living either among clouds or in a room like Rebecca's bedroom in that film, attended by someone as fierce as Danvers. Neither fantasy allows for the odor of the breakfast fish which that day pervaded the apartment near the Marble Arch, though I certainly did not bring in this detail in my increasingly awkward interview with Markova; for it is certainly true that when one tries to make amends for some tacit transgression, the original condition only grows worse. The more I protested, not knowing why, my devotion to red-haired Vivian and dark Doris (tea had segued into dinner in Shepherd's Market and that meal—two veg. and a cut off the joint—into scotch-and-soda back at their apartment) the more remote the ballerina became. I saw her again through the years but only across the room over the backs of Helen and Oregano, the two white china cats. A mystery befitting Drosselmeyer, a rather melancholy one. I had so liked sitting at Markova's pretty feet.

I have mentioned that Leontyne Price was a regular but her husband, William Warfield, was present only twice when I was there. The marriage was then breaking up. The last occasion of his presence may have been a barometer for the weather of that marriage for he made me a proposition I could not accept involving an activity in the bathroom. When the mention of money did not turn the trick I got called, in front of several people, "Young Massa." Considering the alternative, this was like a settlement out of court. Years later in Rome, Leontyne was rude to a friend and me and I always supposed it had something to do with a sense of loyalty to her former husband, though I was by that time, or my star was, setting in the Van Vechten firmament: the musical had flopped. Still, moments of the Roma adventure are worth preserving.

On the Via Veneto my friend and I ran into Price's secretary-companion, a fat young man whose name is not recorded in any of my papers. The diva was in Rome recording opera; I know that Giorgio Tozzi and Rosalind Elias were there also. The second encounter with the secretary brought the surprising news that Miss Price wanted to see me and this message was delivered day after day with some trifling excuse which did not matter to me at all. I was quite happy exercising my Roman feet, as we called them, from sunup to sundown. We dined with Rosamund Elias several nights in restaurants where olive oil was highly featured, starred indeed—so good for singers' throats. Miss Elias, a wonderful artist, exemplified what I had come to expect of opera singers, which was heartiness, an attitude both unassuming and secure, and a sense of humor that embraced bawdiness. Also with us, among us, apparently hounding Leontyne with no success, was the little blonde girl whose baby-sitter Price had once been, whose family had sponsored Price's career to a certain extent. As we had not asked to see Leontyne, my companion and I did not mind not seeing her, but the blonde Southern girl minded very much; her little blue suits and dresses became wrinkled, her big blue eyes more forlorn with defeat. Remembering that Price had once been her baby-sitter, it was an easy step to see the depressed child as a little lamb bleating after a lost ewe. The secretary told us privately that Miss Price had said (and I quote accurately; I wrote it on a napkin that also features the secretary's rather malicious pen drawing of Marian Anderson), "There ought to be a statue of limitations on gratitude." I murmured that there probably was such a statue, on the Palatine. . . .

At last in the lobby of the Excelsior one night, as my friends and I stood admiring Risë Stevens in her scarlet dress, no longer an Octavian but a most ravishing Marschallin, Miss Price swept in, bore down upon us, staring straight into my face; and bore on past carrying like a treasure ship the gold of her eagerness to see us. Perhaps it was after all too precious to spend.

But to speak of the "rilly rilly" great (pace Ed Sullivan), Truman Capote was refused admittance to Carlo's because of his "maliciousness." I put this in quotes for two reasons: I am quoting, and because it is such a fascinating reason in the milieu. I think Capote had given Carlo too much competition in the center-stage department. One of Carlo's dicta to me was that a good host should be self-effacing; this was probably thought of and proffered on an occasion when he needed to subdue me in my own house, still a difficult thing to do. Another bit of advice was *never refuse anything* (ah, William Warfield). I think what he meant was "never refuse to give me anything" for he was then in the midst of a campaign to part me from some beautiful handmade Bohemian (I think) cups and saucers to which I was, in his view, unaccountably attached. I still have them, or the remnants.

The other time that Van Vechten kissed me was more regrettable than the first, the day I thought he was dying on the floor and tried to revive him. There was no excuse for the second kiss, he just grabbed me and stuck his peanut-encrusted tongue into my mouth. Secondhand peanuts are always hard to take but the regrettable part was that this bit of playfulness was witnessed at close quarters by Dorothy Gish. I think my real deep wariness of VV began that night, because of Dorothy, who was more innocent-appearing even than her sister, her little lisp making her seem like a child.

Now, before I press on, having spoken of my dislikes perhaps too frequently, I must detail that I was disliked by a number of people in spite of Van Vechten's belief that all fell before my charm. Brooks Atkinson's wife Oriana, for example, dismissed me as soon as seen, and as though I were a servant— or, as I suspect she thought, the snake in the garden, but this time consorting with Adam rather than Eve. Many people believed that VV and I were lovers. I was always there and my numerous photographs backed me up, so to speak, whenever Carlo left my side, which was not too frequently. But for the record, beyond the two kisses recorded there was no physical contact between us; and this was not due to my reluctance. . . . I was the only person at Carlo's who could cause Zachary

Scott to quit his incessant grinning and look subdued, if he did not in fact frown.

Now it occurs to me, hindsight being surely one of the properties of memoirs, that some negative reactions may have been because of the makeup I sometimes wore. Having a good clear complexion I naturally did what I could to tamper with it. My favorite makeup was 7-A, which I believe was called Juvenile—and I am speaking here of theatrical greasepaint, scarcely the most subtle substance to put on your face. In childhood theatrics when we used burnt matches to draw on mustaches and old-age lines, I had burned one eyebrow almost entirely off and sometimes I would fill in this curious blank with boldly drawn brows of theatrical eyeliner, also greasy. Van Vechten never mentioned the times when I came to his house like a clown (as I think now I must have looked) nor did anyone else ever mention it, not even under the brilliant studio lights with which Van Vechten erased lines rather than retouching his photographs. But now, having become a conservative in that respect (a little face-bronzer in midwinter about does it) I can't imagine why I did what I did, nor how I got away with it. I see myself riding subways made up for the stage, and wonder why I was not jumped on and beaten up. But that's the eternal provincial, the hillbilly, speaking, for in this theatrical town actors do, and often, ride the subways made up, usually after a performance. I've seen Tom Ewell carrying greasepaint on his face, and the aura of Monroe about him, under the mortuary lights of a late subway train.

But as I said, Carlo was never critical of me, not in the early years.

This, however, did change.

Act Two

Both Carlo and Fania specialized in statements and behavior meant to have a shocking effect. When they came to my apartment for dinner Carlo always rode but Fania walked through the Park, blessed days of memory and safety. Fania, arriving and finding Carlo surrounded by women, would shout, "You whores leave my old husband alone!" This could be disquieting to a lady innocent and new to the scene. I should explain that the frequently shouted lines did not always devolve upon theatrical intention, but were due to the growing deafness of both parties. Fania had another tragically impending infirmity that I did not learn about for years.

Once, leaving the opera with the Van Vechtens, we stopped to chat with a famous man-and-wife. She is dead but he, as I write, is still among us, so I will just say that he is one of New York's most respected publishers. Oh, let's call them Alfred and Blanche Knopf. . . . As soon as their backs were turned Carlo shouted that *she* looked like an old prostitute tonight. One observed the slowly stiffening backs of the victims and felt the way the crowd about us subtly shifted their attention from cab-grabbing to us. In tones as ringing as his own had been, Fania questioned Carlo's paternity. This was followed by an exchange of invective that was frightening because of the blood-darkened faces, the apparently genuine rage. The crowd, upon which I morbidly concentrated, seemed mesmerized and one could feel their longing for a knife, a gun, a heart attack. Mob psychology is the same at the Met as in post-midnight Times Square. All at once without transition Carlo made kissing sounds and called Fania in a dulcet coo his naughty angel. One saw then that they had only been amusing each other and did not care what the rest of us thought (or feared).

137

The stiffening back of the victim:

Noguchi turns away from a table at Capri and Carlo loudly announces that he *used* to be very beautiful;

A small, rather humpbacked woman turns away from another table after kissing Carlo's hands and murmuring endearments. Carlo, to the restaurant at large, "The last time I saw ——— she puked on the table."

Or consider the slowly stiffening front of the victim:

At a countertenor recital we are all in the front row. The man is a friend of theirs, Russell Oberlin (whom Carlo wrote to me could have played our Countess as well as anyone). Fania and Carlo are separated by four or five regulars. The tenor sings to a lute, bending over it, lulling it. When the song is particularly soft Fania screams out that Russell looks like a mountain pouncing on a mouse;

An opera singer in quiet recitativo falters to hear what Carlo and Fania think of her costume. The singer is Price, the opera is *The Girl of the Golden West*, and the costume is described at full hoot as "a pair of bloomers." This is followed by maniacal laughter; seven people laughing, unable to stop, can daunt even a woman who believes in statues of limitations. Can daunt even Puccini.

One explanation for the terrible behavior is that scarcely anyone was scarcely ever sober. And yet as much as the youngest of us drank, it was not enough to settle Carlo's distemper on the matter. He once told me, when I had unaccountably refused a drink, that he had not drawn a sober breath until after the age of forty. It seemed like a prescription, a formula for a colicky child.

Let it be understood that all these people mentioned here were Carlo's subjects, many in more ways than one. He photographed us and commanded us, a most benevolent king, much of the time. Among my letters from him I find a collection of faces and bodies on postal cards: Irra Petina, Antony Armstrong-Jones, Pearl Bailey (nude to the waist), Tallulah Bankhead, Markova, Mattiwilda Dobbs, Olivier, Luise Rainer, Gertrude Stein, Jean Marais, Edna St. Vincent Millay. No Elinor Wylie. I may have wanted that one too much; but he was free with anecdotes about her (about anyone, so long as the stories were not serious-minded). About Elinor Wylie he said, "Tell her *The Venetian Glass Nephew* is the best novel you ever read and she will turn her back on you. Tell her she is beautiful and she will follow you anywhere."

These letters and photographs, telegrams and postal cards, are like his voice in my ear telling me: of Alice Toklas's conversion to Catholicism, which upset him and Fania very much; telling me of Marilyn Monroe's intent to divorce Arthur Miller and saying, "she hopes Simone Signoret will be as obliging." He had a passion for Signoret (eccentric, beautiful, and Jewish), who had been his prime choice to play the Countess. Even then, she was growing quite zaftig, but that might have suited Ella Natattorini; the question was: Signoret, an Iowan? When I posed it he would counter with: Margaret Leighton, an Iowan? (for she was interested). Greer Garson most looked the part, and had even promised me "I'll bring you luck, Mr. D.," but I never had the chance to find out what that beautiful woman could do. When our producer fled we were stuck with Irene Manning.

Undoubtedly the flop of the musical, which closed in May 1961 after five performances, affected him deeply. But it was a cheap, distraught, even foolish little production and I cannot, twenty-three years later, talk or write coherently about it. I have it from others that he had expected the musical's success to cap his career, as he put it. He had written this to many

139

people during the halcyon days when we planned scenes to resemble Renoirs, when we, against Iowa tradition, decided to have a boating party on the river, an intricate scene with stars becoming chandeliers and bobbing boaters turning before our eyes into waltzers. One line in the song that spanned those scenes caused him to my helpless dismay to cry. The townspeople are singing as Ella and Gareth, she fifty and he seventeen, step out of their boat and into a waltz:

> Young night embraces
> The fading day
> Like a lover—

Carlo's only letter that I can find with reference to the flop was written the day of the reviews and sent across the Park by messenger. It is filled with concern for me, not for himself, and there are no reproaches. He assures me that his love, and Fania's, will endure. A letter written later that year attests to the continuance of our familiar games: "do not *buy* me a snake."

The only other letter I received about the flop from anyone I had known through Carlo was from Lin Yutang who stuck to the quality of the songs, reminding me that VV had been among our best music critics: "and in music, as in literature, time is the real judge." Given by Dr. Lin, as it were, the choice of professions, I renounced the former and took up the latter. And Van Vechten renounced me.

But not before I had paid some dues. At least that's the way I see it after long years of contemplating it. Otherwise, why the delay? These dues are in the form of public humiliations, too many to go into, for he was not inventive and the sameness of the episodes is boring. Why I endure them, or more than one, is a matter for the analyst's couch, a bed I have

never lain, and will never lie, upon. One example of these
paid dues will suffice.

The place is Le Moal, the exact location within the restaurant is the window with its two tables, a choice spot from
which to contemplate the cold rain edging toward gray snow.
At the other table are two women who look alike. From the
start Van Vechten baits them for he wants the window to
himself, or wants a better audience. Trying to make safe conversation I mention that my hair is growing thin on top. He
says, "You will buy a chestnut wig of hyacinthine curls and I
will lead you around on a thin gold leash set with rubies," and
for the benefit of the puzzled ladies he adds, "nude." Having
their full attention he informs me, "They are mother-daughter
lovers." And they leave, hurriedly, touching in the familiar
agitation of a Van Vechten mark. We drink daiquiris and he
expands upon his theme for the benefit of the new arrivals, a
better audience for they are two men. He grows obscene, his
face mottled red, and to amuse and perhaps disarm him I
improvise a blues riff using his chosen theme of sado-maso-
chism:

> Baby, baby, baby,
> I got news for you
> Baby, baby, baby
> I got news for you
> I'll be anything you want, baby,
> And so anything you tell me to.
>
> I'll be your big fat sassy mama
> And boss you all around
> I'll be your big fat sassy mama
> And boss you all around
> Or get down on all fours, honey,
> And be your poor mistreated hound.

141

He is vastly amused, some of his tears of joy due to the disgust of the two businessmen in our window. "More! More!" he cries, pounding on the table. And I give it.

> I'll lick your boots
> And even higher
> If you tell me to,
> I'll lick your boots
> And even higher
> If you tell me to
> But if you rent me out to other
> mens, baby,
> I'll cry a boo hoo hoo hoo hoo.

And we get very drunk and I don't mind too much the information handed me and the watchful men that I will now have to settle in life for being "a famous typist," for I was then supporting myself by typing for an insurance company, from which I played hooky when he beckoned. There are other digs, none of them leaving very large holes (though I can recall them still). At last we are ready to brave the sleet. At the hatcheck counter, which at Le Moal is (was) just opposite the bar, he zeroes in on the woman in charge, whom neither of us has seen before. Is she not new? and she replies in heavy French accent that she is. Further questions reveal that she is from the Auvergne and, surprisingly, that she is Jewish. At this he tells her in his normal voice, which has become several tones louder than the average, that if he were not in a hurry to get this young man back to his duenna he would come back there and eat her cunt.

I remember the slow swiveling at the bar as customers turn upon their stools; it seems to me that they are as graceful as the Rockettes doing one of those delayed-step routines, but

only now do I see it that way. At the time this is what occurs:
I leave him with the uncomprehending woman and rush
from the bar onto sleety Third Avenue and up, anywhere,
anywhere to get away from the suddenly intolerable person,
the great man of the world gone small. Behind me I hear his
voice calling to passersby: "Stop him, stop that young man!"
I wonder if someone will trip me up as I am the only young
man running pell-mell toward Bloomingdale's. But no one
seizes me and at Bloomingdale's I take refuge from the sleet
storm under the marquee at the entrance to the men's store.
And here he comes, waving his umbrella which he has not
bothered to open. And sidles under the marquee beside me,
among the preoccupied throng also sheltering there. He
addresses them, in a way, through me, at least they pay attention as though addressed. I will not record his speech though
I can recall the words. But the speech ends when he gives me
a prepared-for and carefully thought-out and very public
goose, deep enough to pain my virginity in that place.

Yes, I saw him again. And again. But the night came, as such
nights always do, I suppose, in such circles—perhaps anticipation of such nights is the flocculant for such circles—the
night came when Van Vechten cut me at the opera. I had seen
his group far down front and had no intention of invading
them but was spotted by one who came for me, and when I
got to that place of judgment I was cut. Leaving, I met a
woman gaping in the aisle at the imposing man in the red-
satin-lined opera cape. "Who is that famous person?"—a very
New York question. I told her. But wish that I had said Carl
Van Doren.

When Van Vechten died I read about it in the early morning
Times on my way home from a party. The notice said that he

would be at a certain funeral parlor and I went there and he was not there nor expected. Back at home I called his apartment and Miss Perkins, as he called her—Mildred Perkins, his cook and friend—said, "Lover boy, do you mean he didn't invite you?" I had a moment of fear for her; it sounded as though she were asking if Carlo had not invited me to his own funeral. But she was referring to his assistant. She wept and I did too, a bit. She asked me why I had given them up. Later Fania was to say, "You little bastard, why did you drop us?"

Saul Mauriber, Carl Van Vechten's assistant, compiled and published a collection of VV's photographs under the title *Portraits.* Here some of them are, the regulars and the meteors, in their touching moments, their unguardedness, their beauty. Talent gleams from the surfaces and from deeper within, a combination of Van Vechten's artistry and the brilliancy of so many of his subjects. His photography, like his writing, his style of dress, his music criticism, his life, was innovative and unmistakable. His subjects live on. How they glow.

A couple of years after his death Fania came to dinner. I thought she was being her usual hyperbolic self when she said that she could not see a *goddam* thing and *please* put on more *lights.* When I took her home, to the apartment she had taken on Central Park South when Carlo died, I saw the old drawing room in its effects, but it was like a wild vision as though my first impression had been taken and expanded and parodied, for all the delicate things lay under the light of thousands of watts, not a kindly light to throw upon the past. It was then I realized the degree of Fania's affliction. This expansion of effect, the coruscation, was like the growth of the Christmas tree in *The Nutcracker:* blown out of proportion; and I said good-bye to Fania in this flood of unreality, which actually was no real change at all. She was Clara left forever in the Land of Sweets, in the blaze of marzipan colors, in the tragedy of can't-go-home-again, of blindness.

But the Van Vechtens always managed to have the last word. Fania died in New Jersey in a place called Dun Rovin, a name of the sort that used to inspire her lustiest scorn, and thus one hears her laughter, a whoop aimed at the gallery. It is an announcement to Carlo that the intervening years have not changed her and that she anticipates no changes in him. His naughty angel.

I hope he listened.

V an Vechten was in my estimation too sparing of details from a worldly life. At times it seemed to have been the worldly life for which I had hungered as an adolescent, and which I had tried to bring into at least imaginative being, using images from books as spare parts. With small success. I recall a brown autumn day—the seasons in the wilderness as clear-cut in their boundaries as though sawn out of white pine—when I stood by the mailbox, a brochure, for which I had sent a quarter, in my hands. It was foreign, from Austria. I stood there striving to bring into focus that place of its origin, trying to create the interior of the Rothausplatz pictured therein where, according to the English translation (it was also in German), there were many rooms, restaurants and rathskellers and cafés. For all my efforts on that day of brown-leaved whirlwinds that rose around me like waterspouts, all I could see of an Austrian nightclub was a replica of the splintery-floored café at the town's truckstop, rickety tables with oilcloth covers, bare bulbs, and doorway draped in grease-reeking chintz beyond which was the dormitory where truckdrivers slept with, inside their skulls, inside their dreams, the

146

afterimages of the wide long land that uncurled with the roads.

Van Vechten had been everywhere, lived dissolutely and undoubtedly chastely as well, had mistresses and lovers, been alone and been kept. On this last, only, was he sometimes loquacious (which does not mean informative). However, out of the spare parts I constructed the following.

The Knopfs kept insisting that he meet a particular woman. He kept refusing. One evening when he was invited to dinner chez Knopf he was put next to the woman to whom he spoke not a word beyond the introduction. The mutual boycott (he said it was mutual) continued after dinner. He watched her being helped into her furs, saw her turn to survey the room. When her eyes met his she said "Come, Carl" and he went, and did not leave her for—was it sixteen years? Twelve? She was Mabel Dodge Luhan. She built especially for him, he said, the Villa Curonia in Italy, Fiesole, he said, and furnished it with perfect things from all over the world. Here together they entertained *tout le monde.* Here they parted, in this manner: the house is full of guests, she comes downstairs followed by luggage, bids everyone, emphasis on Carl, enjoy themselves, leaves. Never again to return. Whether they saw each other again or not he did not say, but I prefer to spare them those rueful glances across crowded rooms, an obligatory embarrassment to erstwhile lovers. So I will say that she went to Taos and retired there and that was the end for them.

When I went to Italy for the first time he insisted that I seek out the caretaker of the Villa Curonia and tell him that I was a relative of Signora Dodge, and ask to be shown around. By the terms of her will the villa was kept in perfect repair, in perpetuity. But I could find neither caretaker nor villa, of that name, in Fiesole. Afraid of disappointing him, I said that

147

I had found both, and was enthusiastic (he never asked for details about anything except sexual experiences) and found out only years later that the Villa Curonia is elsewhere—is it Sesto? Stia? Nearby, but not in, Fiesole. A curious lapse. He always said he would never write memoirs and he did not, but I wonder if his various reasons for not doing so were the accurate ones; perhaps the mislocation of the Villa Curonia is the real clue: that he had lost like the moon his memory. (An irresistible allusion. As I write the radio is playing a song from *Cats*, with the words "Has the moon lost her memory?", except that the singer is asking if the moon has lost her "mammary," which makes the next line, "She is smiling alone," of clinical interest.)

All during these days of smart lunches and nights of opera and drawing rooms and parties, a small man could be found hanging around the fringes of Van Vechten's life. He too smiled often alone, with what seemed an attempt at detached irony which translated upon his unprepossessing face as stomachache; he was of that saturninity of complexion that bespeaks hours upon the po po straining, as it were, at a gnat. Some of his labors, which turned out to be a kind of biography of Van Vechten, were published. They are competent, humorless, gullible, and more than a touch sycophantic. If any were published in Van Vechten's lifetime, Carlo did not send me a copy, an oddity in itself for he methodically sent me each word written about him as well as by him, and many of the words written over the years by his friends. My reaction to some of these latter could lead to brief estrangements as when I characterized James Branch Cabell's writing as "pure shit." As for Mr. Kellner's work (the fringe fellow), I do not know if Van Vechten held it in esteem or contempt, only that he kept it from me. I did not see any of it until years after Van

Vechten's death. There is a brief mention of the musical wherein he subscribes to the cliché opinion: good music, lousy book. So what else is new?

Van Vechten had approved, heartily, of my play. He wrote to me that the atmosphere was so real he could float in it. Producers said it read as though it had been refined in performance. But it had not, and in rehearsals lay its undoing. Actors rewrote lines when I was at music rehearsal. I came in to hear the following from Margaret Hamilton, who defected soon afterward: "Now that I've spilled the beans I'd better go cook them." I yelled out, "Who the hell's line is that?" Hamilton went, but the line (and others of her authorship) stayed at the director's insistence: surely the veteran actress knew more about dialogue. . . ? That bean line was singled out by one of the reviewers as an example of my dreadful dialogue. The book director, the dance director, and the musical director did not agree on anything. Songs were truncated, dances dropped (almost entirely; opening night saw one dance, a solo); other songs were eliminated because Irene Manning could not sing them though none spanned more than two octaves. The head money man, who may have been a gangster, wanted the "class" of my material but he wanted it coated with hard Broadway glitter, all the rhinestones that Shubert Alley could disgorge from its old garbage cans. For him, too, a song lyric was dropped because he said it sounded like the guy singing it was a fairy. Here's the lyric, a poem that the seventeen-year-old hero, Gareth Johns, wrote:

> The taste of love
> Is as sweet and rich
> As the taste of honey growing
> When the turtledove sleeps
> On a willow switch

149

And the noonday cocks are crowing,
An evening love
Has the taste of wine
As full to the tongue,
And tart,
But the taste of love
Is bittersweet
In the morning of the heart.

The behavior of union members at rehearsal and during performance was as reprehensible as any I have heard about, and I became for a time a collector of stagehand infractions. An example: engrossed in their backstage card game they failed to move props, so that one living room set had in a corner of it the railroad signal, metronomically negative, from the previous scene.

The scenic designer, drunk from morning to night, constructed some sets too large for the stage, yet he put rich people in tiny rooms with on the walls religious pictures more fitting to poverty-stricken Mexicans.

The costume designer had never consulted old prints or photographs of Worth designs and dressed the Countess like something out of a Watteau painting. It was his work—he is well-known now, a frequent award winner—that drew the only venom Van Vechten spewed upon the production. All else was forgivable, including the mammoth sets, for we had changed theaters in mid-rehearsal, but William Hargate's failure to research his material was too much for Van Vechten and earned his contempt.

The final blow was the discovery of just what hope our star, Irene Manning, had held for the show, for all her daily pronouncements to the press: she had contracted to do a stock *The King and I* only a month after our opening and had been allowed this through unbreakable contract by the former producer, Richard Barr. It was his absurd contract with this voiceless woman, whom he never asked to audition, that forced us to retain her when he left. Though in fairness to whomever I state here that when he went it was at my insistence. I took the show away from him with Van Vechten's approval—at his insistence, really, because Barr had announced yet another delay—and found in the same afternoon my new producer and one of the money men, the one rumored to be a gangster.

Concerning that, all I know is that one 2:00 A.M. I was got out of bed to receive this man and the two others with him, both of them as beautiful as only sin can cause men to be. One was blond and one dark. Both smoked fat cigars. At some point the blond asked me, "How much money do you need, kid?" and from his jacket pocket pulled a gun and moved it to the inner breast pocket. This was right out of *Kiss Me, Kate* and after that I could not have been parted from them.

Through them I met an idol of mine whom they brought to rehearsal. She was tallish and slim, wore a high-necked dress, and was both handsome and plain. She reminded me of someone, perhaps one of my sisters, but I could not settle on it. She was Ann Corio, whom I used to watch with total admiration at the Roxy Burlesque Theater in Cleveland, where my father and I would repair at church time on a Sunday morning, the one thing other than folk music that we had ever shared and enjoyed. (About Lois DeFee, an Amazon stripper, he said, "A man could hang his hat on one of those.") The two beautiful men were involved in putting Miss Corio's show, *This Was Burlesque,* on the boards. From that conversation in the darkened theater among the four of us I see rising like smoke two premonitions involving the beautiful men: the flop of *The Countess* and the great success of *This Was Burlesque.* One premonition is surrounded by a nimbus of pretension, the other is straightforward and clean. The goal of the latter was to make money, and so they did. The goal of the former: to garner some spurious "class" by association, doomed thereby to failure. But I don't think Ann Corio was fooled. She liked a song of mine, though, and hummed along with the reprise. I thought how pleased, how astounded, my father would have been, that I had given pleasure to Ann Corio!

After having said that I would not talk about the musical, I see that I have, but as I am writing it seems more and more that I must justify the atrophying of a large part of myself, a willful act, for if pursued I am confident that that career would have yielded what I wanted of it. I did not pursue it for several reasons, the major one of which is that if I had I would not be alive at age fifty-nine to write however bitterly about it. From my first exposure to them, I have cordially disliked people in show business—cordially, the good word, for I bear them no malice and am grateful to be often so powerfully entertained and moved by their art. But their unreality in their own lives and in the way they touched mine—the touching more than anything like that of ghosts whose matter may envelop yours but without sensation on their part—always appalled me. Even the most stable of them, among whom I place my friend Kim Hunter, are ectoplasmic compared to the civilian: consumed by or consuming some role other than their own; shopping at the A & P is seen as playacting and to attach the necessity of the act to themselves, however loosely like a poorly designed costume, they must imbue it with glamour, relate it to their persona which does not need to eat, or needs to eat like Falstaff. Thus Eileen Herlie performing that simple necessary chore must relate how someone in the checkout line called out in disbelief, "Hamlet's mother at the A & P?" I don't mean to impugn the honesty of Eileen Herlie, but these things never happen when I am there and I am frequently in queues with the famous, this neighborhood running to the likes of Robert Redford and Anthony Quinn, Jackie O. and Mildred Natwick and Eartha Kitt. What I am saying is that all actors—and directors and designers and composers, but chiefly actors—have had to see themselves as seen by others, in the glow of comedy or tragedy or improbability, and I have never been able to see myself as anything other than myself, and that's a big gap. When I slept in the aisle of the theater, too tired to go home, and drank a water glass of scotch to push down the sleeping pills to ensure that I *would* sleep in the charnel house, I saw only myself afraid and alone, hopelessly working on an addiction, and I refer to the sleeping pills and the scotch. It was not a glamorous figure I saw lying there in the darkness in my Gucci suit, pillowing my head on a silk raincoat, though the clothes when bought had been meant to make me glamorous; what I saw was someone headed for failure and heartbreak, bleakness and several kinds of death. My willingness to condemn a genuine talent still fills me with some of the aged horror and despair and I believe I have been punished for it, and can only hope that the punishment is over.

Observing the wreckage of the musical on opening night, Mabel Mercer said to me, "There's no place anymore for Noel Cowards. You should have written music and lyrics, or book, or music, or lyrics. Today the more collaborators there are, the greater the chance of success." But I maintain that it was too many collaborators who killed *The Tattooed Countess*

and those include Van Vechten, who hounded me unmerci-
fully about *getting the show on,* saying he wanted it to happen
in his lifetime. The advice given repeatedly in his letters is: if
the producers (Bowden, Barr and Bullock) could not get it
moving, then find someone who could. Everyone's opinions
and feelings finally were allowed to matter more than my
own, and this was a failure of nerve. If I had had the courage
of my talent I would have got by whatever method a contract
as airtight as Irene Manning's in which the final word on any
matter relating to the musical play would have been my own.
But I wanted to be liked as well as admired.

My most poignant memory of the failure is of going into
Sardi's with Robert Rounseville, on our way to the depressing
little party given by my producers, and Rounseville's tears for
what might have been. It was the second time he cried for
me. The first was at a rehearsal when he and Claire Alexander
broke into tears and I was needful enough to let them con-
vince me that it was because they had been moved. As indeed
they had, but by the obvious ruin before them on the stage
which I could not see; that vision was vouchsafed me only
when I lay alone in the darkened theater when everyone had
gone, waiting for the scotch and pills to knock me out for a
few hours.

Bobby Rounseville and I made our appearance at "my"
party and I played my part. I bowed to the applause of
my friends as though I were Olivier as he had been at the
opening night party for *The Entertainer* when I had been
one of the applauders. But I, you know, bled, and in the night
I turned and turned upon the sheets feeling the stickiness and
congealing cold of actual blood. The terrors wrought in and
upon the heart were scarcely the material for jokes, but one
reviewer, one Taubman, writing very briefly for the *New York*

Times, tried being funny. Only two of the reviewers acknowledged the scope of the music. The *Variety* notice paid heed but indirectly, by saying that the music would have sounded "even better"—without initially stating that it sounded well —if it had not been for the busy orchestrations and terrible orchestra. This terrible orchestra had never learned the busy orchestrations. At final rehearsal some of the cast wept and demanded only piano accompaniment. The union and the theater-owners had seen to it that we had not had time enough to learn our parts.

It was Miss Manning who furnished the evening's coup de grace by holding the curtain for forty-five minutes while she visited in the dressing rooms and tried to allay her own fears, regrets, for all I know, her guilt. One critic, a notorious drunk, left long before the curtain rose. Nevertheless he wrote a review of the show in which the music was called "pindling"; I wonder what his euphemism was for his alcoholic neglect of the work he was paid for.

The Tattooed Countess was no revolutionary work in any large or important sense, but as originally written by me it did not conform to the clichés of the Broadway musical then prevalent, and in its complicated lyrics and overabundance of music (there were twenty-two songs) it certainly prefigured what Stephen Sondheim is doing now. To Van Vechten I was a combination of Gilbert and Sullivan and Cole Porter. But at the time such as Hanya Holm, a choreographer, said, "Too many *words.* Audiences like few words and many repetitions." They were getting a lot of that from what show people called Harold Rome-Rome-Rome, and from Frank Loesser. From Rome they got, "Wish you were here, wish you were here, wish you were here" and "Fanny, Fanny, Fanny," and from Loesser, "Joey, Joey, Joey, Joey, Joey, Joe."

Coleman Dowell

After belaboring it, the moral of this experience remains inside me, or is imprisoned within the material as I have set it down. A curious legacy of this dry birth, or aborted abortion, is that there is still a singing somewhere in me, bright common voices singing bright common songs ("Extraordinary, the power of cheap music" —Noel Coward), and in the midst of writing the most difficult passages in my books I sometimes leave the typewriter and go for a walk and make up a song to express what I have not been able so far to do. Here's one, which helped me to write a slender paragraph of minimalist prose. It will serve to end this recountal of my brief career in show business, and address the theater directly in my own terms of disillusionment and impotency.

No You, No Rain, No Rose

I built a fire in the fireplace
To burn my letters from you,
The sparks flew up from the chimney
And became a part of the
Blue sky
I called it the
you sky.

Now I can read high above me,
When moonlight brightens the sky,
The ways you told me you love me
And each word you wrote is a
far, bright,
A star-bright
Lie.

A Star-Bright Lie

And when it rains—
What falls on those plains
in Spain,
Except your lies?
Flowers spring up with sly
deceitful eyes
Where we walked and laughed together,
Where I loved, alone.

I build a pyre for your flowers
To burn the heart of each rose.
But each time I do there are showers—
And that's the way it goes:
When love becomes a lie
There's nothing true—
No you, no rain, no rose.

Index

159

164